# THE END OF THE SPANISH INQUISITION

In Mexico, towards the end of the sixteenth century, many English Protestants fell into Spanish hands and were tried by the Holy Office. Some met their deaths at the stake.

Philip II set up the Inquisition in Mexico (1569–70) because, he said, he wished to 'free the land which had been made evil by Jews and heretics'.

In 1568 one of Sir John Hawkins's ships, engaged in the slave traffic, was involved in a fight at San Juan de Ulloa, and a party of his men lost their ship and were forced to the land. They lived there in peace for three years, until the coming of the Inquisitors. Then the hunt began for the Englishmen, who were caught and brought before the tribunal. They were beaten through the streets to the applause of the spectators and many of them were sent to Seville that the Holy Office there might deal with them. Seven of them escaped, but the rest of the party who had broken jail were recaptured. Some were burned, others were sent to the galleys.

Jean Plaidy

# THE END OF THE SPANISH INQUISITION

**A STAR BOOK**
*published by*
the Paperback Division of
W. H. ALLEN & Co. Ltd

A Star Book
Published in 1978
by the Paperback Division of
W. H. Allen & Co. Ltd
A Howard and Wyndham Company
44 Hill Street, London W1X 8LB

First published in Great Britain by
Robert Hale Ltd, 1961

Copyright © Jean Plaidy, 1961

Printed in Great Britain by
Cox & Wyman Ltd, London, Reading and Fakenham

ISBN 0 352 302248 8

## NOTE

In order to avoid footnotes, sources and references are given in the text.
My very special thanks are due to the librarians of Kensington
Public Library who have worked so hard and patiently to procure
rare books for me, and thus have aided me considerably in my
research.

# CONTENTS

## RULERS OF SPAIN FROM THE RISE OF THE SPANISH INQUISITION TO ITS SUPPRESSION

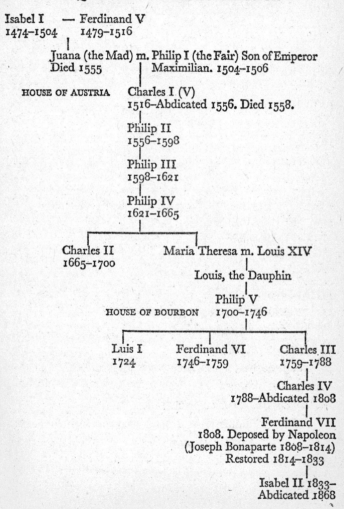

Isabel I — Ferdinand V
1474–1504   1479–1516

Juana (the Mad) m. Philip I (the Fair) Son of Emperor
Died 1555              Maximilian. 1504–1506

HOUSE OF AUSTRIA   Charles I (V)
1516–Abdicated 1556. Died 1558.

Philip II
1556–1598

Philip III
1598–1621

Philip IV
1621–1665

Charles II                Maria Theresa m. Louis XIV
1665–1700

Louis, the Dauphin

Philip V
HOUSE OF BOURBON   1700–1746

Luis I        Ferdinand VI      Charles III
1724          1746–1759          1759–1788

Charles IV
1788–Abdicated 1808

Ferdinand VII
1808. Deposed by Napoleon
(Joseph Bonaparte 1808–1814)
Restored 1814–1833

Isabel II. 1833–
Abdicated 1868

## CHAPTER ONE

# THE COUNCIL OF BLOOD

During the second half of the sixteenth century Spain was ruled by the most notorious of all her kings – Philip II – and partly because the country had reached a certain stage in her development, partly because of the character of the strange man who sat upon the throne, the Inquisition flourished to such an extent that it dominated the country.

Philip was the most powerful sovereign in the world, but the burdens which had been laid upon his slender shoulders were too much for him, and his eventual failure was due to an absence of imagination and the inspired genius necessary in a great ruler, not to any lack of conscientious devotion to duty.

There was no monarch in the world who had a higher sense of duty; it was no fault of his that his mind worked slowly and that he was constantly finding himself a move behind his opponents. His father had taught him to govern; he continued to follow his father's methods, although Emperor Charles would have been the first to point out that other times demanded other methods. Philip, lord of half the world, suspicious of all, unlovable, secretive and above all bigoted, was not a strong enough man to fill the role of most powerful monarch in the world.

He was determined to establish the Catholic Faith in all countries under his dominion; and there was no country which suffered more agony, on account of this desire of his, than the Low Countries.

This tortured land which was, unfortunately for its people, under Spanish rule, clearly desired to be a Protestant country; and it is not in Spain that the Protestants were persecuted so bitterly (for Protestantism had never had a very firm hold in that country) but in the Netherlands.

The Emperor Charles, born in Flanders, was more Fleming

7

than Spaniard; yet he was guilty of trying to force Catholicism on a people who were prepared vigorously to reject it.

Strangely enough Charles, presiding over the Diet of Worms, had, when Martin Luther stood before it, been instrumental in bringing about the latter's escape. It is true that Luther had been given a safe conduct, but that was no guarantee of safety; it was not difficult to find means of wriggling out of promises. However Luther had been allowed to state his beliefs and escape.

Charles later regretted this and thirty years after the event, at the time when he was abdicating in favour of Philip, he actually stated that he had committed a grave error by not allowing Luther to be sent to the stake.

However he set about rectifying that so-called error very soon after he had made it; as it was in his power to fight Lutheranism in the Netherlands, he did so with enthusiasm.

An edict was proclaimed forbidding the people of the Netherlands to publish Lutheran books, and the penalties for disobeying this rule were very severe indeed. In 1522 Charles appointed Councillor Francis Van der Hulst of Brabant to be Inquisitor-General of the Netherlands. Van der Hulst, like many before him, practised such cruelties that had he not escaped in time he would have paid with his life.

It was necessary, after the rule of Van der Hulst, to suspend inquisitorial activities for a while, but Charles was determined to destroy Lutheranism in the Netherlands. We find him fiercely demanding the death penalty for all heretics, by 'the sword, the ditch and fire'.

These orders were carried out. It mattered not what nationality the victim, it was only necessary for him to be a Protestant to be submitted to the utmost cruelty.

Our own William Tyndale, whose great crime was that he had translated the New Testament into English, was one of them. He had been exiled by Henry VIII and worked in great poverty in Antwerp. He longed to return to England but Henry refused him permission to do so. In the year 1535 he was lodging at the house of Thomas Poyntz, an English merchant who was very interested in the Lutheran theory. Unfortunately, he was betrayed to the authorities as a dangerous heretic and consequently was arrested and taken to Vilvorde, a strong castle fortress near Brussels, where he was kept for fourteen months.

He had friends in England and Thomas Poyntz was working busily on his behalf. This man went to England and begged Cromwell to intercede for their countryman. Poor Poyntz, not only were his efforts in vain, but he himself was arrested and imprisoned for heresy. But he was more fortunate than Tyndale and succeeded in escaping.

Meanwhile Tyndale remained in prison, calm, very ready if necessary to wear the martyr's crown. He believed firmly that the Bible was for the use of all, and he was ready to die to give it to the people. He was known among the little band of exiles as a man of great virtue. Each Monday he visited all those exiles who were in need, and out of his small wealth aided them to the best of his ability; on Saturdays he acted in the same way towards any destitute people he found in the streets of Antwerp. This benevolence was made possible by those merchants of this city who, sharing his views and being determined to uphold the Protestant Faith, clubbed together to make him an allowance. We are told that the whole of this allowance was devoted to the needs of others.

It was this man who, on the 6th of October, 1536, was taken from his dungeon to the stake. He showed no fear but quietly awaited his fate, and he is reputed to have said as the ropes were bound about him: 'Lord! Open the eyes of the King of England!' Rule, in his *History of the Inquisition*, writes that he was burned alive; other historians state that he was strangled before the faggots were lighted. Rule, being fiercely Protestant, is inclined to paint the Catholics in as dark colours as possible.

In 1522 the Augustinian Friars of Antwerp declared their belief in Lutheranism. Several of them were burned alive, singing psalms until the smoke choked them. One was tied in a sack and thrown into the Scheldt.

These terrible sentences did not deter the noble people of the Netherlands. They welcomed the Lutheran ideas and, once they had accepted them, could not be turned from them. As the years passed and Philip took the place of his father, persecution became more fierce, and it was the custom to burn the men and bury the women, alive.

But Rule records several accounts of horrible punishment under Charles. In 1524 a sailor, who went aloft in a ship lying at anchor in the port of Antwerp and preached Lutheranism to the crowds who gathered on the shore to listen to him, was arrested, handed to the secular arm, put into a sack and thrown into the river.

Several priests were burned alive because they believed the new ideas and had married. There is one account of a family of six – father, mother, two daughters and two sons-in-law – who were all burned alive together because they had accepted Lutheranism.

One of the most cruel practices was to take women who were about to give birth to children and burn them at the stake during the birth. This, says Rule, was the fate of several women in Holland.

The people of the Netherlands seemed to be inspired rather than deterred by these horrific sights. It may have been that they found Protestantism a religion suited to the national character; it may have been that they were a people who had for years learned to make their own decisions. They had always discussed new ideas and, if need be, criticized their rulers. They were not a people to lie down meekly and accept a certain doctrine because their rulers had decided they should.

The soil of Flanders was to be saturated with the blood of martyrs in the years to come when the Spanish Inquisition in all its fury was set up in that freedom-loving land. Even at the time of Charles's retirement to Yuste it is calculated that his victims had numbered between 50,000 and 100,000. In retirement at Yuste and reviewing the situation he wrote that he wanted to establish the Spanish Inquisition in the Netherlands that he might prevent heresy spreading from Germany, France and England. He had come to the conclusion that all who had fallen into heresy should be condemned to suffer death by fire and their heirs the confiscation of their property. He admits that the people were outraged by the severity of this treatment, but insists that he was compelled out of necessity to act as he had.

And when Charles decided that he had done with the world and would end his life in retirement at the monastery of Yuste, he handed over his crown to his son Philip.

The Netherlands had suffered mildly compared with what was to come.

When the Inquisition was set up in the Netherlands the resentment of the people was intense. How different these Netherlanders were from the people of Aragon who, at the time of the assassination of the Inquisitor Pedro Arbués, instead of making a stand beside those who had risen in revolt called for their blood.

These people of the Netherlands were determined to fight for the right to worship God as they pleased. Discontent reigned in the land and the more rowdy elements of the population seized the opportunity to show their disapproval. Thus in August of 1566, three hundred people, clubs and axes in their hands, entered the churches in the neighbourhood of St Omer and set about demolishing those images so beloved by the Catholic community. From St Omer they went to Ypres where they attacked the Cathedral. Menin, Comines, Valenciennes, Tournay and finally Antwerp were dealt with in their turn.

News of what was happening spread through the country, and riots broke out in big towns such as Rotterdam and Haarlem and, when the soldiers were called upon to take up arms against the rioters, they refused to do so.

It was naturally the uneducated mob who took part in these riots; they went into the pulpits and mimicked the Catholic priests; they put on their robes and made obscene gestures; they placed the images of the saints against wooden stakes and set fire to them. Valuable books were burned; and it was calculated that the damage done to Antwerp Cathedral alone was about four hundred thousand ducats.

When news of the rioting reached Brussels the Regent of the Netherlands declared that the country must be defended against those who sought to destroy its religion.

This Regent was Margaret, Duchess of Parma, who was an illegitimate daughter of Emperor Charles, and therefore half-sister to Philip. Her mother had been Margaret Vander Gheenst who when she was seventeen had caught the roving eye of the Emperor. The fruit of this liaison was brought up by Charles's aunt, who was herself then Regent of the Netherlands. Charles however, as he showed later in the case of Don John of Austria, was not one to forget his children, illegitimate though they might be; and Margaret was royally educated. When she was twelve she married Alessandro de'Medici; fortunately for her Alessandro died a year after the marriage.

Later she married Ottavio Farnese, a grandson of Paul III, and Charles benignly bestowed upon her the Duchies of Parma and Placentia as a dowry, doubtless to make up for the fact that, although Margaret was then a young woman, her new bridegroom was a child of twelve.

In 1559, when Margaret was thirty-eight, she became Regent of the Netherlands, an office bestowed on her by her half-brother, Philip II of Spain.

There was however much opposition from the noblemen of the Netherlands to the threatened curtailment of religious liberty; and the three most prominent of these were Egmont, Hoorne and Orange. And of these three it was William of Orange who became one of the great figures of history.

He was born at Dillemburg in Nassau on the 25th of April, 1533, of Lutheran parents, and in his early days he was educated in that faith. This did not please Emperor Charles, so when the boy was twelve years old he took him from his parents that he might be brought up by his, Charles's, sister Mary, as a Catholic.

William was so outstandingly intelligent that the Emperor was attracted by him, and when he was fifteen he took him into his own household as one of his pages. Charles came to have a great affection for William and entrusted him with many delicate missions; at the famous abdication ceremony it was on William's shoulder that he leaned; and he asked Philip to make use of the services of this brilliant young man and see that adequate rewards came his way.

There can be no doubt that Charles regretted that William was not his own son; his attitude to William would doubtless have been different had he been able to look into the future and see in William the great leader who was, in time, virtually to free his suffering country from Spanish tyranny.

William in his turn had a great respect for Charles. The Flemings revered their Emperor for, harsh though he could sometimes be, they felt that he was one of them. It was when Philip – so essentially a Spaniard – stepped into his shoes that they showed their resentment.

William married Anne of Egmont, daughter of the Count of Büren, when he was eighteen; she died a few years after the marriage and he then made an alliance with Anne of Saxony, a rich heiress and an earnest Lutheran, which caused consternation to Philip, who had by that time taken his father's place. This marriage broke up after thirteen years, when Anne returned to Germany. The fact that it was most unsatisfactory may explain why William was inclined to indulge in amorous adventures.

In spite of his love of gaiety and courtly manners he was far from free and easy in his behaviour; he was known as 'William the Silent', for he spoke little, although when he did so he could be very eloquent. His perfect manners and gallantries enhanced his popularity with his fellow countrymen; and the fact that he never allowed his tongue to betray him was a great advantage in his political life. William the Silent was very adequately endowed with the qualities necessary to the great leader he was to become.

There was one other quality he possessed – perhaps the finest of them all. He was vehemently against persecution and earnestly supported the right of all men to worship as they pleased.

It was said of him by a contemporary writer that he was known as a Catholic among Catholics and a Lutheran among Lutherans; and it may have been that in his great fight against Spanish tyranny he became a Protestant; but what William the Silent really fought for was the freedom of his people.

Had he been a bigot it is doubtful whether he would have been such a fine leader. Philip's eventual failure was in a large measure due to his bigotry; and it is interesting to compare his failure and that of his wife, Mary I of England (another bigot), with the success of Elizabeth I, a queen who may in secret have murmured 'A plague on both your houses', while in public she could give the impression of being the friend of all.

Meanwhile in Spain Philip was kept informed of what was happening in the Netherlands. 'By the soul of my father,' he is reputed to have said, 'this shall cost them dear.' He kept his word.

The time had come, Orange knew, either to fight or to flee, and as he was not in a position to do the former, being a wise man he left the Netherlands. The rebels were brought to order and Margaret restored temporary peace to the land. She was not however prepared to forgive those who had risen against Catholicism, and she inflicted terrible punishment on the offenders. She sent her troops across the country and wherever they discovered those of the reformed faith meeting together, they rode among them deliberately trampling them under the horse's hoofs, shooting them or taking them to execution. In many cases there was no trial; those suspected of the slightest interest in the reformed faith were hung up on gibbets; and all over the countryside these gruesome spectacles were to be seen.

Meanwhile Philip had decided to send the Duke of Alva into the Netherlands at the head of the army; and the blood bath was about to begin.

This very successful general was already noted for his harshness even before he came to the Netherlands; and what his coming was to mean to that persecuted land was clear when he wrote to Philip that his aim was to have every man feeling that at any hour of the day or night his house might fall about his ears.

As soon as he arrived in the Netherlands he established his garrisons in the important towns. The soldiers were given great licence and there is no need to state the nature of the cruelty and indignities heaped upon the inhabitants. Contemporary writers tell us that the oppression of the Spaniards was great and that anyone who possessed something which the Spaniards desired was immediately accused of heresy so that what was coveted might be confiscated.

The people were filled with panic and many left the country by stealth, taking with them all they possibly could.

Egmont and Hoorne were arrested. William of Orange had shown his astuteness by leaving the country. Cardinal Granvelle, whose experiences in the Netherlands make it clear that he knew what he was talking about, said when he heard of the arrests of Egmont and Hoorne: 'But have they drawn the Silent

One into the net?' And when he was told that Orange had escaped, he answered: 'Then if they have not caught Orange, they have caught nothing.'

Alva's first task was to call together a tribunal which was to be invested with extraordinary powers and was to investigate the recent riots and bring those responsible to justice. It was called the Council of His Excellency and was made up of twelve judges; one of these was the notorious Juan de Vargas, a vicious man capable of great cruelty. The Council was called by the people of the Netherlands: 'The Council of Blood.'

The persecution began; the great need was to bring victims before the Council of Blood. So the familiar methods were used. Husbands and wives were induced by threats to inform against each other, as were children against their parents; if they would not do so, they were introduced to the rack and the hoist and those other devilish persuaders. Those who were suspected and remained in hiding had their names posted up in the streets, and criers paraded the towns shouting that they were wanted and that any who knew where they were and did not inform against them were themselves suspect. On the night of Ash Wednesday, 1568, five hundred people were arrested in Brussels in the middle of the night, dragged from their beds to prison – all to be condemned to death.

A common enough sight in the streets was that of people being seized, pinioned and dragged away. If the victims were poor they were hanged without delay.

Some were beheaded, many were hanged; others were burned alive at the stake. 'Condemned to die' was the order of the day; the method was left to the judges who were often the uneducated and mercilessly cruel soldiers. It was understood that any man or woman who was a steadfast Lutheran merited the more terrible death by fire.

One exceptionally cruel practice was to burn the tip of the tongue with a red-hot iron. The swollen tongue was then compressed between two plates of metal which were screwed tightly together. The sufferer was taken to the scaffold where he – or she – was to be hanged or burned alive. In acute pain it was very probable that the victim would be unable to suppress his groans which, with his swollen tongue between the pieces of metal, would sound like some strange language. This was intended to add to the amusement of the spectators.

Alva and his lieutenant, Vargas, appear to have enjoyed exercising their cruelty on these people. Vargas is reputed to have shouted when awakened from sleep: 'To the gallows! To the gallows!' Words which when awake he used so frequently. As for Alva, in his letters to Philip he gives an impression of licking his lips over his achievements. 'I am going to arrest some of the richest and worst offenders, and bring them to a pecuniary composition.' 'I have reiterated the sentence again and again, for they torment me with their enquiries whether in this or that case it might not be commuted to banishment. They weary me of my life with their importunities.' These comments are revealing, betraying as they do Alva's cynical attitude towards the misery he was bringing to thousands and an almost fiendish delight that it was in his power to do so.

Again we have an example of the stupidity of the bigots. The cities were being deserted and the Netherlands was fast losing that prosperity which its flourishing merchants had brought to it before the Inquisition was introduced into its midst. Thousands escaped into Germany where a refuge was gladly given to them.

Margaret had abdicated. She believed that the leaders of the revolt should have been punished, but she considered this attack on the people to be foolish as well as cruel. She went to Parma and there lived in comparative obscurity until her son Alexander Farnese became Governor of the Netherlands, when she was at his side.

De Thou asserts that Philip, aware of the criticism of many countries, sought to justify the action which Alva was taking in the Netherlands, and put the case before the Inquisition in Madrid.

The tribunal's verdict was that all who were guilty of heresy, apostasy or sedition, and those who, declaring themselves to be good Catholics, had done nothing to bring heretics to justice, were guilty of treason both to Church and State. The penalty for such crimes was well known; and as the people of the Netherlands, with very few exceptions, had committed this crime, they were all condemned to death, and their property was to be confiscated. That they might serve as an example to all in the future they were to have no hope of grace whatever.

Prescott doubts the authenticity of this story, although he admits that it has been repeated many times by writers to whom it does not occur to distrust it. He says: 'Not that anything can be too monstrous to be believed of the Inquisition. But it is not easy to believe that a sagacious prince like Philip II, however willing he might be to shelter himself under the mantle of the Holy Office, could have lent himself to an act as impolitic as it was absurd.' (*History of the Reign of Philip II.*)

When the Emperor Maximilian protested to Philip and asked him to put an end to persecution in the Netherlands, Philip replied: 'What I have done has been for the repose of the Provinces, and for the defence of the Catholic Faith. Nor would I do otherwise than I have done, though I should risk the sovereignty of the Netherlands – no, though the world should fall around me in ruins.' (*Correspondence of Philip II.*)

Thus spoke the bigot, and it is gratifying to record that his conduct was to set his empire tottering. Even at this stage the exiles from their county were rallying round the man to whom they looked to save them. At Dillemburg William the Silent was making plans.

There were two unsuccessful expeditions, one led by the nobleman Hoogstraten and the other by Villers, but at Heyligerlee, Louis of Nassau (brave brother of William the Silent) won a victory over Alva's forces. This was wonderful news for the suffering people, and Alva's fury was boundless. The Counts Egmont and Hoorne were beheaded; and William and his brother Louis were sentenced to perpetual banishment, and their estates were to be confiscated.

It was impossible, of course, to carry out the threat to exterminate the entire nation, but Alva's tyranny and the execution of great leaders like Egmont and Hoorne, did for a time appear to have the effect of subduing the people. So that three years after Alva's arrival in Flanders he felt justified in proclaiming a free pardon for all those Flemings who would now become faithful subjects of Philip II.

According to Hume (*Spain: its greatness and decay*) it was not religion which made the Flemings revolt against the Spanish yoke so much as their love of money. Philip had levied the *alcabala* on all sales and purchases; this was ten per cent which went to the treasury. It was the merchants who had made Flanders wealthy, and they were not prepared to see business deteriorate because of such a tax.

Philip had been accustomed to draw on the Flemish bankers for loans; they now declared that, owing to the conditions imposed upon trade, they were bankrupt and could no longer supply the King with money. Philip at this stage began to question the wisdom of Alva's rule. Protests were coming in from all over the world; and, perhaps most important of all, Alva had his enemies in Madrid, the chief of whom was Antonio Pérez who was later to figure in one of the most dramatic cases connected with the Inquisition.

In 1573 Alva was recalled to Spain, a disgraced man who had failed in his mission, which was to subdue the Netherlands and make the people docile vassals of Spain. We are told that his disgrace almost 'broke Alva's heart' – an inadequate punishment for the misery he had brought to thousands.

His place was taken by Don Luis de Requesens y Zuñiga whose orders were to pursue a more conciliatory course.

Protestants were persecuted in the Netherlands with greater ferocity and with more frequency than anywhere else, for in this case the Inquisition was working against an entire nation; and in Spain Protestantism, apart from the two outbreaks at Seville and Valladolid, was rare.

It is not know how many people suffered during Alva's command. It was, naturally, impossible to eliminate the entire nation of some 3,000,000; but Alva is reputed to have boasted that, during his term in the Netherlands, he was reponsible for the death of 18,600 people, and that about 60,000 left the country in order to escape him and his bloody-minded assistants.

## CHAPTER TWO

# ENGLISH CAPTIVES OF THE INQUISITION

It is not surprising that, when the Spanish fleet failed against England in 1588, the country rose with a mighty determination and, lacking the great galleons, and the finer military equipment of the would-be conqueror, struck the first great blow which was to shatter a mighty empire.

The English knew that the intention was to set up the Inquisition in their land. They were aware that English sailors who had fallen into the hands of the Inquisition had been tortured and murdered for their faith. The fact that some humble sailor – who might have been a friend or relation – had been brutally murdered, was enough to bring home to them the menace which threatened them.

There was danger of falling into the hands of Spaniards when sailing the seas or trading in the towns of Spain. A chance word, a book which was carried, might bring a charge of heresy. There would be the arrest, the imprisonment and the hopelessness of being far from home with no help at hand so that the torture chambers and burning at the stake would very possibly be the outcome.

English merchants in 1576 brought a petition to the Queen, protesting against the treatment received in Spain; and later the behaviour of the Inquisition towards English merchants and sailors was the cause of much diplomatic activity; but the Holy Office was adamant. Those who did not adhere strictly to the Catholic Faith were heretics whatever their nationality and therefore worthy only of death.

The Catholic Church was desperately afraid of Lutheranism. The power of the new Church could not fail to be appreciated and it was fast becoming the most formidable rival Catholics had ever known. It has been said that but for the Inquisition the Catholic Faith could not have survived, that for this reason the former was necessary and its cruelties must be forgotten. Determined to keep Protestantism from Spain the government placed the harbours under the control of the Inquisition. One of the rules, quickly brought into force by the Holy Office, was that ships coming into harbours should be searched and, if any heretical book were found, the crew was to be taken before the tribunal.

This rule had been established during the reign of Henry VIII, but Henry was not the man to stand aside and see his sailors treated in such a way; he immediately protested to the Emperor Charles who, at that time wishing to remain on good terms with the King of England, withdrew the rule.

Philip was different from his father. There were times when his bigotry could carry him beyond the realm of reason. Under Philip, if an English Bible or Prayer Book were found in the possession of an English sailor he was arrested, brought before the tribunal and perhaps sentenced to a term at the galleys if he denied his own religion; and if he did not deny it, it was the stake for him in a 'fool's coat' – the English ironical term for the *sanbenito*.

In the year 1565 twenty-six English subjects were burned at the stake in Spain, and ten times as many were lying imprisoned awaiting a similar fate. Sir John Smith was sent on a special mission to Philip to make complaint about this, but the mission was unsuccessful.

This seizing of Englishmen was not confined to Spain alone; for Spain was in possession of a large part of the world, and every sailor who left his native land was in danger not only from the elements and chances of fights at sea but – most dreaded of all – the Spanish Inquisition.

At an *auto de fé* in the Canaries (which, though discovered in 1402 by a Norman sailor, Jean de Bethencourt, had eventually fallen into the possession of Castile) an Englishman, George Gaspar, appeared in the year 1587.

He had been arrested on suspicion of heresy and taken to a prison in Tenerife, and whilst there had been seen to turn his back on the crucifix as he knelt in prayer. On being asked why he did this, he replied that he addressed his prayers to God and not to images. This was asking for trouble and it was not denied him.

He was taken before the tribunal, where he admitted that he was a Protestant, and then cruelly tortured; but nothing could make him deny the faith in which he had been brought up. He was a self-confessed heretic, quite impenitent, and there was only one course open to the Inquisitors. He was handed to the secular arm and condemned to be burned at the stake.

George Gaspar was undoubtedly a very brave man, but he was determined to avoid that agonizing death at the stake; at the same time he was equally determined not to deny his faith. He had managed to hide a knife in his prison and, when he heard that the terrible sentence had been passed on him, he plunged this into his stomach.

Unfortunately for him he did not die of the wound, and the Inquisitors piously declared that it was the will of God that this wicked man should not escape his just punishment on Earth. He was dying, it was true, but there was still time to let him feel the fire. He had to be taken to the *quemadero* on a litter and the flames hastily lighted, so that he might die in the utmost agony.

Even if prisoners escaped burning at the stake, other punishments were inflicted which must have been almost as hard to bear. There was one man, whose case is recorded under the name of John Reman (presumably Raymond), who was an English sailor and had been brought before the tribunal of the Holy Office in the Canaries. He was imprisoned and whilst there was discovered discussing Lutheran theories with other prisoners. He was immediately brought before the tribunal, vigorously questioned and taken down to the gloomy torture chambers. He was racked so cruelly that he was ready to admit anything that was asked of him and, declaring his wish for reconciliation with the Church of Rome, escaped death. He was 'pardoned' but his punishment was to be two hundred strokes of the lash and ten years in the galleys. When one imagines the prolonged hell of the galleys, quick burning at the stake seems almost preferable.

At the same *auto* there appeared the crew of the ship *Prima Rosa* which had been taken by the Spanish. This crew consisted of eleven Englishmen and one Fleming. They were imprisoned and tortured, and all, with the exception of one who died while in prison (no doubt due to the hardship imposed upon him), declared themselves converted to the Catholic Faith. They were 'forgiven' but their punishment was a hundred lashes and sentences to the galleys.

It was particularly infuriating to Englishmen to know that the oars of the Spanish ships were in many cases manned by their own countrymen.

A cousin of Sir Francis Drake, John Drake, was arrested in South America after a shipwreck; he was obliged to appear at an *auto de fé* as a penitent, which must have been excessively galling for Sir Francis.

In 1594, one year before the death of Sir John Hawkins, his son Richard became a prisoner after an action at San Matteo. Many of his crew were, without trial, sentenced to the galleys, but Richard with some of his senior officers was taken to Lima, there to be brought before the Inquisition. None of them, it is recorded, was so firmly Protestant as to be burned at the stake; and in his book, *The Spanish Inquisition,* Cecil Roth points out that the member of this party who stood most firm in his faith, and was consequently sentenced to perpetual imprisonment, was named Leigh, as was the famous character in *Westward Ho!* So perhaps it was the records of this particular case which fired the inspiration of Charles Kingsley.

William Gardiner, a Bristol man, came before the Lisbon Inquisition in the reign of Edward VI. He was, we are told, 'Honestly brought up and by nature given to gravity.' He was a small man but very handsome and 'in no part so excellent as in the inward qualities of his mind'.

He was employed by a merchant whose business connections were in Spain and Portugal; and when William was twenty-six he was sent by his employer to Lisbon to complete some transactions.

There were several Englishmen living in Lisbon, and these were Protestants. William made their acquaintance on his arrival and spent a great deal of time in their company.

On the 1st of September, 1552, a royal marriage took place in Lisbon, the King's son marrying a Spanish princess, and

William, who had mingled with the crowd sightseeing, for the first time in his life saw Mass celebrated. He watched incredulously while the Host was elevated and the people knelt, and it seemed to him like a pagan rite. As he left the crowds and went silently to his lodging, he came to the conclusion that he must point out to all those people that, in behaving as they did and bowing down to images, they were giving way to superstition.

He was so concerned about all this that he felt he must do something. He knew that public protest would almost certainly mean painful death for him, yet he felt himself forced to act.

The festivities of the wedding continued, and when Mass was again celebrated, he found a place near the altar; when the King himself entered the church and Mass began, William took a Testament from his pocket and began to read it. The Host elevated, the people fell to their knees, but William merely sat reading his Testament. Then suddenly he ran to the Cardinal who was officiating and, snatching the Host from him, he threw it to the ground and stamped on it.

There was consternation which for the first few seconds showed itself in silence; then the people fell on William and would have torn him to pieces, if the King had not commanded that he should be released. His was a case for the Holy Office.

The King then approached William and asked why he had done this.

William explained that he was an Englishman in this country on business, and went on to say that when he witnessed such idolatry he could not endure it.

He was handed over to the Inquisition, and his English friends were arrested, also. Before the tribunal he talked freely of religion and his fearlessness astonished all who came into contact with him.

He was submitted to torture. The Portuguese were more brutal than the Spanish yet less disciplined. Behind the Inquisition in Spain was a fierce determination to wipe out heresy; in studying the methods used in Portugal it often seems that the Inquisitors did not care so much whether heretics were reconciled to the Church of Rome as that a spectacle was provided for the people. In Spain any criticism levelled at the Inquisition would bring the critics to immediate examination and almost inevitable death; in Portugal, however, possible changes in the methods of the Inquisition were openly discussed. Yet for all their carelessness the Portuguese appear to have been what would seem impossible: that is, more cruel than their neighbours in the Iberian Peninsula.

William Gardiner suffered many kinds of torture. One of these was to have a ball forced down his throat, then violently jerked up; this was repeated again and again until he was in a state of collapse. But whatever tortures they applied or threatened, William remained adamant and declared that if he had the chance he would behave in exactly the same way as he had in the cathedral.

His tormentors lost their patience with him. When they cut off the right hand which had seized the Host and thrown it to the ground, William seemed to delight in his suffering, for he picked up the bleeding right hand with his left and kissed it.

He was then taken out into the streets that the large crowd of spectators might enjoy his further sufferings. In the market place his left hand was cut off. He was then set upon a donkey and carried to the river's edge where the stake was set up. But this was no ordinary stake which had been prepared for the man who had insulted the Host. Attached to it was a rope and pulley; and when the faggots at its foot were lighted William was hoisted above the flames and lowered into them. Up and down he went, so that his agony might be protracted and that the people might see him slowly roasted to death.

All the time he was suffering this indescribable agony he was answering the people who called to him, and quoting psalms and passages from the Bible. 'When Christ ceases to be your Advocate,' he is reputed to have said, 'then will I pray the Virgin Mary to be mine.'

He continued thus until the rope was burned through and his body fell into the flames. (Rule's *History of the Inquisition.*)

The case of Isaac Martin is more often quoted, perhaps because he escaped from the Inquisition and published his own account of what happened to him.

Isaac Martin arrived in Malaga in the year 1714 with his wife and four children; and when he landed and his goods were searched at the Custom House, a Bible and certain books of devotion were discovered in his baggage. These were confiscated because, he was told, they must be examined to see whether they contained anything against the Holy Catholic Faith.

He lost the books and after two or three months' residence in the city he was summoned to appear before a court where he was accused of being a Jew; because his name was Isaac and one of his children was called Abraham this was reckoned to be very suspicious. Several of his neighbours were brought up for questioning and they all agreed – no doubt because it was expected of them – that he was a heretic. His position was a very dangerous one, for he was liable at any time to be seized by the Inquisition as a heretic; and if he were practising Judaism his position was even more dangerous, for Jews were not allowed to live in Spain or Portugal unless they became Catholics.

For four years nothing happened, but the Inquisitorial eye had not ceased to watch Mr Martin. An Irish priest, he tells us, made his life intolerable by calling continually upon him in order to make him turn Catholic. Isaac could see that there was to be no peace at Malaga and planned to sell up and return to England.

His friends shook their heads warningly over this, because they knew that if he attempted to move he would be seized by the Inquisition which, while it allowed him a little licence – as a cat will a mouse – would not allow him to escape altogether.

One night, when he and his family had retired, there was a knocking on his door, and before opening it he saw from a window that several people were standing there. He asked what they wanted at such an hour and was told that they wished to come in. 'Come back in the morning,' replied Isaac; 'I do not open my doors at such an hour.' They broke open the door and, to his horror, Isaac recognized the dreaded *alguazils* and the priests and familiars of the Inquisition.

Bewildered he asked what they wanted and was told that their business was with the master of the house. 'I am the man,' Isaac answered, and was told to get his cloak and come with them. Isaac then said that he was an Englishman and that the Inquisition had nothing to do with him. He said that if they had anything to say to him they could say it after he had given notice to his Consul which as an Englishman he was entitled to do.

They shook their heads. Apparently he knew little of the methods of the Inquisition. Meanwhile his wife and children, hearing the commotion, came to see what was wrong. Terrified they clung to him and implored the officers of the Inquisition for mercy. Such scenes were of course too familiar to these men to have any effect on them. Isaac was dragged away to prison, and his wife and children turned out of the house that it might be searched for incriminating evidence.

The poor woman and her children had nowhere to go; and their terror at finding husband and father taken from them and themselves turned into the streets at night can well be imagined. Fortunately a kind friend took them in, and the keys of the house were not returned to Mrs Martin until five days later when, returning to her home, she found all the family's possessions had been taken away, and there was nothing there, as Martin says in his account, but 'the bare walls'.

After four days in prison, Isaac was told that he was to go before the Inquisition at Granada. He begged to be allowed to see his family before he went, but this was forbidden. He was fettered and set on a mule, and thus he left Malaga while the people gathered about him calling out that as a Jew and an English heretic he deserved to be burned.

As Isaac was fettered and the mule on which he rode was loaded, riding was difficult; as the fetters hurt the mule's neck the animal took the first opportunity to throw its rider and Isaac was pitched upon a rock. His back was almost broken so that he had to be lifted back on to the mule, and thus very painfully journeyed to Velez-Malaga.

Here he had a stroke of good fortune, for an English merchant who knew him well saw his arrival and insisted that a doctor should dress his wounds. This was a great comfort to Isaac who was able to ask his friend to look after his family and, if he were murdered by the Inquisition, to see that they were able to get back to England. This the friend promised to do and it was suggested that coach or chaise be procured to take Isaac into Granada as he was in such pain; but his guard said that this was impossible as only a mule could be used on the rough roads. The friend provided mules and provisions and all the comforts he could think of, and Isaac and he took a sorrowful farewell for they were fully aware of the fate of those who fell into the hands of the Inquisition.

Isaac records that it took three days to travel the seventy-two miles from Malaga to Granada, and that his physical agony was only exceeded by his mental torture.

When they reached Granada he and his guard put up at an inn, for it was day-time and, writes Isaac, they put nobody in the prison of the Inquisition by daylight. He was allowed to write to his wife, but he says that his wife did not receive the letter, and the purpose in suggesting he should write it was doubtless that he would in some way incriminate himself.

As soon as night fell he was taken to prison and put in a dungeon. His jailer asked him what his religion was and, on Isaac's answering that he was a Protestant, he was told that he was then no Christian. He was warned that he must be very quiet in his cell and not speak, whistle or sing; and if he heard anyone cry out or make any noise he must remain silent. Any sound from him would be rewarded by two hundred lashes.

He was given some bread, a little wine and half a dozen walnuts and told to undress and go to bed. It was very cold in the cell, the floor being bricked and the walls two or three feet thick. In one of these walls was a hole a foot long and five inches broad, but owing to the thickness of the walls little light came in.

In the morning Isaac was told to dress and get his provisions. He was given half a pound of mutton, two pounds of bread, some kidney beans and some raisins, with a pint of wine and two pounds of charcoal.

In his cell he had an earthen stove, some earthen plates and a few pitchers; he had a wooden spoon but no knife, fork nor table. He also had a broom with which to sweep the floor.

He was told that the food was to last him three days and then he would be given more. A doctor was allowed to visit him, for the pain in his back was acute, and he was bled and given oil for his back and allowed to stay in his bed.

He was eventually taken to an audience and describes the

room in which were two men, 'one sitting between two crucifixes, the other on his left with pen, ink and paper'. He was bidden to seat himself upon a stool provided for this purpose.

Asked if he could speak Spanish, he told them that he could, and was questioned concerning his religion. He was a Protestant, he said; and he was then questioned about his birth – in London – and his religion. He was then told that he had been brought up in the dark but that he might enlighten himself if he desired to do so.

When he was asked if he did not worship the Virgin Mary and the saints he replied that he believed the Virgin Mary was the mother of Jesus Christ carnally, and that the saints were happy, but he did not worship them. He worshipped God in three Persons and nothing else.

The Inquisitor then said that it was a pity England had left the true Faith and fallen into heresy. Once the country had produced great saints; now it produced nothing but schisms and heresies. When Isaac said that he believed England was producing men as good as it ever had he was promptly told to hold his tongue.

The audience over – it had lasted an hour – Isaac was told that his case was not hopeless and could be remedied; and a week later he was again taken before the Inquisitors, more questions were asked and when this audience was over he was returned to his dungeon; after that there were many other audiences.

The Inquisitors cajoled and threatened. Isaac quotes them as saying: 'You have been brought up in heresy; it is a pity. You were all good people and good Christians in England till Henry VIII came; and that was your first loss. Then came Queen Elizabeth, and she was a very wicked woman; that everybody knows; and here of late you have had one that you call King William; he had no religion; what he aimed at was to get the Crown; and so you have been led away.'

Again and again Isaac was taken back to his dungeon, and again and again he was brought before the Inquisitors. This was the well-known pattern of wearing down the victim; at the audiences he was questioned and cross-questioned, and reminded that there were means of saving the souls of heretics.

These dark hints at torture filled Isaac with apprehension, for his state by this time was very weak, suffering as he had for so long the rigours of prison life and the continual anxiety as to the fate of his family.

During four months Isaac was subjected to fifteen audiences. He was then moved to another dungeon which pleased him at first because it was lighter than the one he had left and he was able to hear a cock crow in the morning and some dogs bark. It must have been wonderful to feel again this contact – small as it was – with the outside world. Moreover in the first dungeon he often heard other prisoners groaning in agony and he presumed that they had been suffering under the hands of the torturers. However the new dungeon, he tells us, was infested with bugs which made sleep impossible during the night.

Twenty-six weeks after he had come to the prison he was taken from the cell with some ceremony, having first been blindfolded. He was led to a chamber and there stripped of his clothes. All this time he was in mental agony, because he believed he was about to be tortured; but it turned out that all this meant was an examination to discover whether he had been circumcised. This was typical of Inquisitorial methods, for these men were well aware of the efficacy of mental torture.

As he had not been circumcised, Isaac hoped this would count in his favour; and so it seemed, for a month after this, one of his jailers came to him and told him he was to be released. He thought this was a further torment and begged the man not to make such jests, but he was assured it was no jest and that the barber was coming to make him presentable. Isaac was so overcome that he could only cry weakly.

When he was ready he was taken to an audience chamber where many people waited, all dressed in ceremonial robes; a rope was put about Isaac's neck and he was made to kneel. He was told: 'Your case has been seen and examined; go along with these gentlemen. You shall soon be released.'

He was taken to a church, in a procession of about forty people, and set on an altar facing the pulpit. A priest mounted the pulpit, carrying papers in his hand, and read out an account of Isaac's misdeeds. 'The Holy Inquisition had done what she could in admonishing me to embrace the Holy Faith of the

29

Church of Rome, without which no man could be saved,' wrote Martin. 'But I was such a pernicious heretic that I would not hearken to the salvation of my soul, and that the Holy Tribunal had found me a great enemy to the Holy Faith.' The priest went on to say that for the crimes which Isaac had committed the Lords of the Holy Office had ordered him to be banished out of their Christian dominions upon pain of two hundred lashes and five years in the galleys if ever he returned to 'these Christian parts'; and having made this pronouncement he gave the order that Isaac was to receive two hundred lashes, which should be applied in the streets of the city.

After this ceremony Isaac was taken back to his dungeon where he was told that if he changed his religion he would escape the lashes. His answer was that he had endured so much that he would suffer this little more.

Next day the executioner came with ropes and a whip, and Isaac was told to take off coat, waistcoat, wig and cravat. His body was put through a collar which was fixed about his waist, hands tied together, and a rope placed round his neck. He was then led into the streets where great crowds had assembled to see the punishment bestowed on an English heretic. The priest read his sentence, ending with the words: 'And so let it be executed.' He was put on an ass and led through the streets, the executioner whipping him with a scourge made of leather thongs as they went, while the people threw refuse at him, crying out that he was an English heretic and no Christian.

Isaac, who was no coward, spoke to the people asking them what country he was in, and when they said he was in a Christian country, he retorted that such conduct was surely not that of Christians, and that they behaved as did the people of Barbary. This sobered the people and made many of them so ashamed that the pelting was considerably diminished.

When the whipping was over, Isaac was taken back to his dungeon and there he asked for brandy with which to bathe his back. This was supplied by his not unkindly jailer; but he was in great pain for some time and unable to lie on his back; but this did not trouble him as much as his anxiety as to when he was to be allowed to leave.

After a fortnight he was told that he was to be taken to

Malaga, there to await a heretic ship. He was once more warned that he was never to return to Spain; to which, naturally enough, he retorted that he had no wish ever again to set foot on Spanish soil.

He was told then that he must take an oath that he would keep secret what had happened to him, and not reveal anything of what he had seen or heard during his incarceration by the Holy Office. (An oath which Isaac felt justified in ignoring. Indeed he may well have felt it his duty to warn Englishmen of the calamities which could overtake the visitor to Spain.)

In Malaga he was fettered and put in the common jail. His wife came to see him, and he told her to make immediate arrangements to get him aboard a ship.

At last he was on an English ship, but a few hours after he went aboard, war was declared between England and Spain, and the ship was taken by the Spaniards and all in her put into prison.

Poor Isaac must have felt that he would never escape, but an official of the Inquisition came to him and told him that as they had ordered that he should not be allowed to stay in Spain, out of Spain he would go, for he was not fit to live in a Christian country. The prisoners were told that Isaac Martin was a dangerous man, being a heretic, and that none of them must have any communication whatsoever with him.

Isaac eventually went on board a vessel from Hamburg and waited for his wife who was trying to get back some of their possessions of which they had been robbed. But Isaac was told that they were very foolish to hope for this or to make any requests, for although Isaac and his family had suffered great hardship, when they considered the cases of others, they must realize that they had been very fortunate; Isaac, being such a stubborn Protestant, might so easily have been burned at the stake.

As the Inquisition had threatened to take one of his children to be brought up in the Catholic Faith (and Mrs Martin had hurriedly had the child smuggled to England) Isaac made her hastily bring the rest aboard. Meanwhile, she was given a little of what had been stolen from her, although, says Isaac, 'they gave out that they had returned us everything.'

So Isaac Martin came home to England. He ends his narrative with the statement that several bishops and clergymen advised him to publish his narrative and that he is 'following their advice'.

Isaac's story makes pitiable reading but in view of what happened to so many at the hands of the Inquisition, there is no doubt that he escaped very lightly.

How fortunate he was that this happened in the early eighteenth century! Under Philip II Isaac would have suffered hideous torture and almost certainly have been burned at the stake. He would never have lived to tell the tale and give us such a comprehensive picture of the methods of the Inquisition.

In his account of his trial and sufferings Isaac Martin gives a description of the Inquisition of Granada, and as it is a particularly vivid one, I will give a brief paraphrase of it here.

The Inquisition, he says, is like a palace until you open the doors of the dungeons.

Built after the style of a convent it had galleries all round it, and the Inquisitors had their apartments in the building. The dungeons were on the ground floor and 'up one pair of stairs and two pair of stairs'. They were fifteen feet long and ten feet broad, and there were two doors to each dungeon; they numbered about a hundred and the prisoners did not share them. Twice a week the prisoners were let out to collect their allowance of food and 'throw out their dirt'. He gives an account of the provisions allowed him, and they seem at this time to have been fairly adequate. Isaac states that he grew very lean but remained in good health.

Prisoners were not allowed books, pen, ink or paper, and however long they were incarcerated were forbidden to receive letters from their families. They must not hear sermons or Mass, and if they prayed they must do so inaudibly; if they were heard they were chastised.

The chief of the prisons of the Inquisition was situated in Madrid; and this was the headquarters, for all prisons in other parts of the country must give an account of their affairs to that one in Madrid.

The Holy Tribunal of Granada was (continued Isaac Martin) almost as large as our upper House of Parliament, and in it hung some very fine pictures. There was also an altar and a throne of red velvet. The Inquisitors sat in decorative arm-chairs which were placed before a large gold-embroidered crucifix, on the right of which was the triple crown and beneath it the cross keys; on the left was a naked sword, and under it the King's arms.

The table was covered with red velvet, and on this table stood a gilded crucifix two feet in height. The secretary sat at the end of the table and the prisoner on a stool before the crucifixes. (From *A Review of the Bloody Tribunal; or the Horrid Cruelties of the Inquisition,* by John Marchant and others.)

As Isaac Martin was brought into this chamber some fifteen times, it would seem that his description is likely to be an accurate one.

From Limborch we hear of the fate of an English woman in Lisbon. She was Elizabeth Vasconellos who was born in Devonshire to the wife of a certain John Chester. When she was eleven years old her uncle, David Morgan, of Cork, who was a doctor, decided to settle in Jamaica. He arranged that he should take Elizabeth with him and treat her as his own daughter.

This was in the year 1685, and as their ship neared Jamaica it was attacked by two Turkish ships. There was a fight during which David Morgan was killed. The ship managed to elude the Turks and put into Madeira, but without her uncle the young girl did not know what to do, for she was penniless in a strange land; fortunately a merchant named Bedford, hearing of her plight, took her into his household as a servant, and here she remained for eleven years.

In 1696 she was married to Cordoza de Vasconellos who was a doctor living in the island.

For eight years she lived happily; then her husband had to leave her to visit Brazil, and while he was away she became very ill. She had always been a Protestant, but during her illness the sacrament had been given her, although she knew nothing about it; on her recovery she was told of this and assured that consequently she had changed her religion and must now acknowledge herself as a Catholic.

This she refused to do, whereupon she was made a prisoner and after nine months was sent to Lisbon to appear before the Inquisition.

Everything she possessed was taken from her and she was put into a cell about five feet square and there left for more than nine months.

During the first week or so she was given only bread and water and wet straw to lie on. When she was taken before the Inquisitors she declared that she had been brought up as a Protestant and that she would remain in that religion. They told her that she had accepted the Roman Faith, and if she denied it she would be sent to the stake.

She was then sent back to her cell, and a month later was again brought before the Inquisitors. Persisting that she was a Protestant she was stripped to the waist and whipped with knotted cords.

Fifteen days later she was once more taken before the Inquisitors. A crucifix was set up and she was commanded to go down on her knees and worship it, and when she refused to do this was told that she would be burned alive at the next *auto de fé*.

Again she was sent back to her cell, and a month later was brought up for re-examination. This time a more severe punishment was inflicted. Her breast was burned to the bone with a red-hot iron in three places. She was returned to her cell with no ointments or bandages to help ease the pain of her wounds.

When a month later she was brought before the Inquisitors who demanded that she accept the Catholic Faith or burn, she answered boldly that she was English and a Protestant and she doubted not that she would be protected if her condition was known to the English who lived in Lisbon. She was ready for the stake but not to renounce her religion.

She was told that any English heretics living in Lisbon would be damned, and since she seemed eager for the fire she should taste it before she was called upon to face the great ordeal.

She was put into a chair and her legs and arms were bound.

A doctor was brought in that he might warn her tormentors how far they could go without killing her. Then her left foot was bared and an iron slipper, which had been made red hot, was brought in. Her foot was put into this and when the flesh had burned to the bone and she lay unconscious, the doctor ordered that the torture be stopped for her life was in danger. So she was taken back to her cell.

Later she was yet again brought before the Inquisitors and her back laid bare while she was savagely whipped. She was threatened with more terrible tortures than had yet been inflicted, and told that if she would sign a paper they would set before her she would be given her liberty.

Now in a state of mental daze produced by so much physical agony Elizabeth signed and gained her liberty. She was told that she would be wise to avoid English heretics; and all her goods which had been taken from her were kept by the Inquisition. She was then turned adrift 'destitute of relief', goes on the account, 'but what she received from the help and compassion of charitable Christians.'

It is comforting to know that there were a few of these living in Lisbon at that time.

Elizabeth's deposition of what happened to her is witnessed by John Milner and Joseph Wilcocks, and is dated Lisbon, 8th January, 1707. (*History of the Inquisition*, Philip Limborch.)

In Mexico towards the end of the sixteenth century many English Protestants fell into Spanish hands and were tried by the Holy Office. Some met their deaths at the stake.

Philip II set up the Inquisition in Mexico (1569–70) because, he said, he wished to 'free the land which had been made evil by Jews and heretics'.

In 1568 one of Sir John Hawkins's ships, engaged in the slave traffic, was involved in a fight at San Juan de Ulloa, and a party of his men lost their ship and were forced to the land. They lived there in peace for three years, until the coming of the Inquisitors. Then the hunt began for the Englishmen, who were caught and brought before the tribunal. They were beaten through the streets to the applause of the spectators and many of them were sent to Seville that the Holy Office there might deal with them. Seven of them escaped, but the rest of the party who had broken jail were recaptured. Some were burned, others were sent to the galleys.

It was because Englishmen and women roaming the world were often brought before the Inquisition and subjected to torture and death that the Holy Office was known throughout England as the great enemy of Protestants. This was so, of course; but many people forgot the sufferings already endured by Jews and Moors, which were even greater than those inflicted on Protestants.

Through the years men and women from many countries were brought before the Spanish Inquisition, in spite of fierce protests from the nations involved.

Oliver Cromwell demanded liberty of conscience for Englishmen in Spain that they might worship God as they pleased in their private houses and that there should be freedom of trade with Spanish possessions. For these concessions he offered alliance with Spain against France. But his offer was declined, the Spanish Ambassador replying in amazement that Cromwell, in asking such concessions, asked for 'his master's two eyes'.

This state of affairs continued, much to the detriment of Spanish prosperity. Thus through the years accounts continued to reach England of the sufferings inflicted by the 'Dogs of the Inquisition' on English Protestants.

## CHAPTER THREE

# POLITICAL USE OF THE INQUISITION BY PHILIP II. THE CASE OF PÉREZ

Philip II had made it clear that he did not intend to use the Inquisition as a political weapon; he was determined – as fiercely as his great-grandmother, Isabella the Catholic, had been – to maintain a Catholic Spain. It is difficult to sort out Philip's motives; he could deceive himself and tell himself that he was determined to save the souls of his subjects for God, when he was at heart concerned to keep them loyal to the crown.

Apologists for the Inquisition are delighted to tell us that it was a political instrument used by the State. Thus they exonerate the Church from association with this much hated institution; and it must be admitted that those in authority were ready enough to use the Inquisition in a political issue, if the opportunity arrived.

Continually in Spain the Inquisition threatened to become a weapon in the hands of the Sovereigns; it brought great financial gain to the exchequer. Philip received through the Inquisition all the galley slaves he needed to man his vessels because 'condemned to the galleys' was one of the most frequent minor penalties.

In fairness to the *Spanish* Inquisition it must be said that it was not put to political service as frequently as the Inquisition in other countries had been. The case of the Templars springs to mind as one of the most flagrant examples of a monarch's using the Inquisition for political purposes. Philip of Spain could never be so blatantly dishonest as his namesake of France had been in the barbarous affair of the Templars.

In the case of Joan of Arc, whose death was of paramount importance to the English, it had been necessary to call in the aid of the Inquisition in order that she should be brought to the flames. Joan had been taken prisoner by the Bâtard de Vendôme, a follower of Jean de Luxembourg who was second-in-command to the Duke of Burgundy. Joan, as a valuable prisoner, would have been worth a very big ransom, for it was the custom for those who greatly desired a particular prisoner to offer a large sum to the captor; and as Joan was calculated to be worth more than five hundred fighting men, the ransom would have been very high indeed. But the English were in a state of near bankruptcy and of even greater fear that the French would provide the ransom money and take the prize. They were eager to have her condemned as a sorceress – for they believed she was one – and for this she could be judged by the Church. According to the law, sorcery was one of the crimes which came under the jurisdiction of the Inquisition; and shortly after her arrest Martin Billon who was Vicar of the Inquisitor of France demanded that she be surrendered to the tribunal.

This was France in the fifteenth century, and Philip the Fair had, more than a hundred years ago, clipped Inquisitorial power so that Jean de Luxembourg, who was very reluctant to hand over the prize, made no haste to do so.

It was then that Pierre Cauchon, Bishop of Beauvais, who, although French, supported the English, was told that since Joan had been captured in his diocese he must, in his episcopal role, demand that she be delivered to him for trial; and once again the surrender of Joan was demanded on a charge of idolatry, sorcery and other matters concerned with the faith. However a large sum had to be raised before Joan was handed over, and the Regent, Bedford, was obliged to impose a special tax in order to raise it.

Joan was forced to stand trial as a heretic and eventually was sent to the stake wearing a paper crown on which was written: Heretic, Relapsed, Apostate, Idolator.

The *Spanish* Inquisition was never so blatantly used for political ends. Archbishop Carranza aroused the enmity of his political enemies and thus suffered unjust imprisonment, but his case cannot be compared with those of Joan of Arc or the Templars, those victims of the medieval Inquisition.

There is, however, a notorious case in the records of the Spanish Inquisition in which it was used to bring a man to disaster, not because of his heresy but because of political scheming. I refer to that of Antonio Pérez.

Concerning this case there is a mystery which has never been satisfactorily cleared up; and as there is a possibility that it may have touched Philip, not only politically, but emotionally, it possesses a romantic appeal which no doubt accounts for its having become one of those cases which are resurrected from time to time by various writers who seek to provide the solution. There is, though, another reason why the case of Antonio Pérez is significant in the history of the Inquisition: this is because of the effect it produced in Aragon.

One theory is that Antonio Pérez was the illegitimate son of Gonzalo Pérez, a cleric, who was in the service of both the Emperor Charles and Philip. There is some disagreement about the date of Antonio's birth. Many writers give it as 1534, but Gregorio Marañón insists that it was 1540. The date has little significance, for whether Antonio was six years older or six years younger would have made no difference to his fate.

His mother was Doña Juana de Escobar, a young woman of Madrid. It was not certain whether she was a married woman – and that again is unimportant.

What was of the utmost importance was that Gonzalo, having been ordained, could not marry, and therefore a son provided a certain embarrassment. Antonio was sent to the country to be brought up, and Gonzalo, who visited him frequently, must have been very proud of him, because he was exceptionally handsome and intelligent. He was known as Gonzalo's nephew and was legitimatized by Emperor Charles in 1542, although this fact was kept secret for many years. That part of the country in which Antonio was brought up was Val de Concha in the district of Pastrana, and Pastrana was in the heart of the estate of Ruy Gómez de Silva, the Prince of Éboli, favourite of the King and one of the most important men in Spain; thus was Antonio brought to the notice of the Prince and Princess of Éboli.

Another theory is that Antonio was the son of Ruy Gómez. It was said, when Antonio was on trial, that he visited the household of Ruy Gómez with great frequency and in that house was treated as a member of the family. In appearance Antonio resembled Ruy Gómez more than Gonzalo Pérez, for Antonio was short of stature, very handsome, slender and lithe, and possessed of a great power to charm. All these qualities were possessed by Ruy Gómez, while Gonzalo Pérez was thickset and completely lacked that suave charm.

Moreover the great interest and favour shown by Ruy Gómez for the young man might indicate that he had a very special reason to seek his advancement.

But Antonio himself never made any reference to the possibility. He is quoted as saying, when Ruy died in 1573, that he felt his death deeply for Ruy Gómez was to him as a father. But surely a very common expression such as this could have naturally been said about one who had been such a good friend to him, as Ruy undoubtedly was. Moreover he referred to Gonzalo Pérez as 'my father and master'; and all through his life he appears to have shown the utmost love and reverence for him.

So, the life of Antonio Pérez began in mystery.

Gonzalo Pérez – and perhaps Ruy Gómez – apparently determined that the young Antonio should be given the best possible education, and he was sent to universities in Spain, Flanders and Italy; in addition to this Gonzalo himself gave the boy tuition. He was clearly destined for a high place in state affairs.

When his education was complete, there were Gonzalo and Ruy Gómez ready to see him launched. Ruy Gómez no doubt saw in him a useful adherent to his own party which was in direct opposition to that of the Duke of Alva, for Gómez, suave, polished and humane, was the natural enemy of the bloodthirsty soldier and persuaded the King to a peaceful policy, whereas Alva fervently believed in fire and the sword.

Antonio, the protégé, was brought to the notice of Philip who was attracted by the young man, and when in 1566 Gonzalo died, it seemed natural that Antonio, who had now had a certain amount of experience under Gonzalo and Ruy Gómez, should take his father's position as one of the King's secretaries.

But meanwhile Antonio had been sowing a few wild oats; and Philip could be prim. There was a young girl at Court, Doña Juana de Coello; she was neither rich nor beautiful, but she became enamoured of the handsome Antonio who was at this time indulging rather freely in love affairs. Juana was no doubt one of many and when she became pregnant and marriage was desirable, Antonio drew back. If he was amorous, he was also ambitious, and there is no doubt that, as the protégé of a man of such power as Ruy Gómez, his prospects were so brilliant that a dazzling match was not an impossibility. He refused to marry Juana and the child was born.

Ruy Gómez disapproved of this callous behaviour; Philip did so even more strongly. Juana was a lady of the Court, and Philip abhorred scandal. So when the name of Pérez was laid before him as successor to his father, the King retorted that he expected those who shared his secrets to present a virtuous front to the world.

In view of such disapproval in high places Antonio consented to marry Juana who was to prove such a noble woman and such a devoted wife to him in his misfortunes.

Thus at twenty-eight Antonio took on the office of Secretary and from the beginning he won the King's favour. Of all his secretaries Philip selected him for special favours. Moreover he worked very hard; he was determined to succeed, and very soon mastered state matters to a degree which was a continual delight to Philip. He had acquired the art of subtle flattery; he paid flowery compliments and made even the humblest with whom he came into contact feel that he was aware of them.

Antonio Pérez was possibly of Jewish extraction and there was in his nature a love of ostentation. He was highly intelligent, he had the King's favour, and on the death of Ruy Gómez he was on the way to becoming the most important minister in the kingdom; it is understandable perhaps that he should have wished to flaunt his wealth and power.

In the year 1575 he rented one of the most magnificent houses in Madrid in the Plaza del Cordón. He filled it with valuable pictures and exquisite furniture; his servants were dressed in rich materials and were taught to behave not as lackeys but as gentlemen, so that his guests were uncertain of their status. Even the horse he rode was perfumed.

But eventually he decided that the mansion in the Plaza del Cordón must be merely his office, and he built another just outside Madrid. In this new house the beds were of silver; and on his own bed he had silver angels fixed and the words 'Antonio Pérez sleepeth: enter softly' inscribed there. It was said that he possessed the most magnificent house in the whole of Spain. Ostentatiously he named it La Casilla (the Cottage).

It was not possible for a man to reach such eminence, and to make such displays, without arousing the enmity of many. For all his suave charm, Antonio's enemies began to spring up all about him.

He needed a great deal of money to live in the style which was so dear to him. As Secretary of State his income was 200,000 maravedís a year and he received another 100,000 as Secretary of Castile besides a warrant for 150,000. This was wealth, but he needed even greater wealth and so he found other means of increasing his income. He was not the first to accept presents for the good he could bring to those who wished to make use of his influence; but it was sometimes necessary for him to pay others for services required.

He was a gambler; his debts were huge; but he continued to live like a Prince and in much more lavish style than that affected by the hermit-like King.

Antonio's position was dangerous; moreover he had come under the influence of his patron's widow, the Princess of Éboli.

Ana Mendoza y de la Cerda Princess of Éboli was a member of the famous Mendoza family, a great-granddaughter of Pedro González de Mendoza, Archbishop of Toledo, who in the reign of Ferdinand and Isabella had played a part in shaping Spain's destiny and had been known as 'the Third King of Spain'. The Archbishop's position in the Church had not prevented his having several children, and one of these was Diego who was born to a lady-in-waiting who came to Castile from Portugal with Juana, the wife of Henry IV. Eventually after a glorious military career Diego married Ana de la Cerda the granddaughter of the Duke of Medinaceli. The son of this marriage married Catalina de Silva, sister of the Count of Cifuentes, and their daughter was Ana who was to marry Ruy Gómez and become the Princess of Éboli.

In 1552 when Ana was twelve years old a marriage was arranged for her with the Portuguese Prince who was then thirty-six. The marriage was, however, not consummated until Ana was nineteen.

After they had lived together as husband and wife for four-teen years, during which Ana had borne Ruy six children (and had had four miscarriages) Ruy died. He was fifty-seven, Ana thirty-three, and she already had a reputation for immorality and lust for power. Ruy's gentle strength and excessive charm, it has been said, kept her subdued during his lifetime; but she is reputed to have shared in his councils and had a firm place in his political life. It was hardly likely that a woman such as Ana would be content to be relegated to obscurity on the death of her husband.

Ana is one of the most intriguing figures of the sixteenth century. As there had been an accident when she was quite a young girl during a fencing match with a page, and she was never seen in public without a silk shade over her right eye, it is extraordinary that she should have been considered such a beauty. Perhaps it was her personality, her charm and vivacity which were so attractive. Yet according to some accounts she was a very difficult woman, and Ruy had greater trouble keep-ing her in order than he did in managing the affairs of the country. The Count of Luna said that Éboli 'covered up a thousand trespasses of that irate and terrible woman'. And St Teresa, who was entertained by the Ébolis at Pastrana, writes that Ana caused her a great deal of trouble which the mildness of the Prince put right.

But when the Prince died and Ana no longer felt his guiding hand, there was certain to be trouble at Pastrana. Ana, deter-mined to call attention to herself, on the very day that he died made up her mind that she would enter a convent. Imperious as ever she did not wait to consider this move but left that very evening for the Monastery of Pastrana, wearing the habit of the Discalced Carmelites, riding through Pastrana in an open cart that the whole neighbourhood might be aware of what she was doing. The people stared in astonishment to see their Prin-cess, usually so sumptuously clad, dressed in a nun's habit. That was what Ana wanted; her gestures appear to be dramatic in the extreme. But though it might have been interesting for the countryfolk to see their Princess thus, it was very disconcerting for the Prioress, Mother Santo Domingo, who, we are told, wrung her hands and cried out that there would be trouble in her house when the Princess entered it.

She was right. Ana had brought two servants with her and for a day or so she obeyed the rules, but then her imperious nature revolted. She refused to speak through the grille and wished to summon people to her cell when she wanted to speak to them; and eventually she retired to apartments at the bottom of the garden and had a door made to open on to the street, so that she could be in contact with the outside world.

St Teresa was angry and threatened to remove the nuns from this convent; and eventually Philip ordered Ana to return to her family and estates for, he said: 'She is more obliged to do that than be a nun.'

Ana was certainly not going to live in seclusion at Pastrana. She looked for a new outlet for her tremendous vitality, and she found it in Antonio Pérez, who, on the death of Ruy Gómez, was perhaps the King's most favoured minister.

Popular legend has it that they became lovers; and this seems a reasonable supposition when the reputations of both these people are considered. Antonio was the hero of many amorous adventures; Ana has been accused of having many lovers. There was undoubtedly a partnership between these two; surely it was, besides a political one, a sexual one.

Consider the lusty Ana still young at the age of thirty-three. It is almost certain that she would have looked for a lover, and because she wished to use Antonio as a means of regaining the power which had been hers while Ruy lived, that did not mean that she would not take him as a lover. Ana was a woman of the world and, if she wished to lead Antonio by the nose, she would have been aware how much more easily she could do this if there were a sexual bond between them.

Gregorio Marañón, who prefers the theory that there was no love affair, says that the story of this intrigue has spread because 'the public loves history to be as like a Vaudeville as possible', and that 'when historians give themselves free reign, serial story writers are left absolutely nowhere!'

Yet when all the known facts are considered it seems that a sexual-political intrigue is far more likely to be correct than a merely political one; and that in this case the Vaudeville, and far more interesting, situation is the true one.

However, no one denies that an intimate relationship of some sort grew up between Antonio Pérez and the Princess of Éboli.

Meanwhile Don John of Austria had been sent to the Netherlands as Viceroy in an effort to placate that turbulent country which had suffered so much under the rule of Alva.

Don John was a wise choice. He resembled his father, the Emperor Charles, more than Philip did; he was fresh from the victory of Lepanto (1571) and was greatly admired throughout the world.

Don John had been born in Ratisbon in 1547, the result of a love affair between Emperor Charles and a beautiful Flemish girl. In his early years John had lived the life of a village boy, educated somewhat scrappily by the village priest. When he was seven years old he had been sent to the household of Luis Quixada, a steward of Charles's household. Charles did not forget him, and commanded Philip to look after his half-brother, which Philip, always a stickler for duty, tried hard to do.

There is a pretty story of their first meeting which had been arranged to take place in a wood. There for the first time Don John beheld the King, his half-brother. Philip is reputed to have taken John in his arms and told him that he was descended from a great man and that the Emperor Charles, 'now in glory', was the father of them both. Philip decorated him with the insignia of the Golden Fleece, and buckled a sword to the boy's side, after conferring a knighthood upon him. The peasant had become a prince.

Don John lived up to his romantic beginnings. He grew to be handsome and charming. Tall and fair he was a great soldier, excelled at the jousts, and was attractive, kindly and beloved. He was, naturally, not without ambition.

Philip, by nature suspicious, must have been somewhat wary of a young man such as Don John. Prince Carlos, Philip's son and heir to the throne, had died in mysterious circumstances, and it was possible that Don John had his eye on the crown. Respected and loved, he would have been a welcome heir. He was regarded as a hero, for after Lepanto he had conquered Tunis. There was one thing he greatly desired and which Philip stubbornly refused to grant; Don John wished to be known as 'Highness', which would have been tantamount to the cancellation of his illegitimacy.

When Don John had taken Tunis, Philip had ordered him to dismantle the bastion La Goleta and set up the son of Muley-Hacem as King. Don John, however, disobeyed the King's orders and instead left a garrison in the fortress, hoping, so it was believed, that one day he himself would be the ruler of Tunis.

When some months later La Goleta and Tunis were lost by Spain, Don John was blamed, and so for the first time in his young and successful life Don John had suffered defeat.

But when he went to Madrid Philip received him with kindness. Perhaps Philip found it easier to be kind to the handsome young man who came less triumphantly than usual; and the next year, on the death of Luis de Requesens, he sent him as Governor to Flanders. Don John took with him as his secretary Juan de Escobedo, a man who, like Pérez, had been a protégé of the Prince of Éboli.

Don John did all in his power to win the Netherlands to his side by following a more gentle policy than his predecessors. William the Silent however had already determined to free his country of the 'Spanish vermin', and there was war.

Don John laboured under great difficulties; he was surrounded by spies who, fully aware of the suspicion with which Philip regarded his half-brother, reported every thoughtless word of the young Prince. Don John began to realize that he had been given a hopeless task and that he, whose efforts had always been so glamorously successful, was now heading for failure. He longed to leave the Netherlands, and he wrote to Pérez suggesting that as the King did not enjoy the best of health and the heir to the throne was but a child, would it not be a good thing if he returned to Madrid and helped to shoulder the responsibilities of the crown.

This, to the suspicious eyes of Philip, seemed dangerous

thinking; and Pérez did not hesitate to show Philip the confidential letters from Don John. Pérez was at this time eager to be friendly with John while he continually made Philip aware of his own loyalty. If by any chance John's dreams were realized Antonio Pérez wished to stand as high with him as he had with Philip.

Meanwhile John needed funds to continue in Flanders, and he despatched Juan de Escobedo to Madrid to explain to the King his desperate need.

Pérez had warned the King that Escobedo's mission to raise money was a blind, and that he had actually come in order to stir up revolt in Castile in favour of Don John against Philip. Philip thereupon gave Pérez secret orders to have Escobedo put out of the way.

Pérez decided on poison, which would be simple as Escobedo was a frequent guest at his house. He thereupon called in the services of three of his servants: Diego Martinez, his steward, Pedro de la Exa, his astrologer, and Roderigo de Morgado, his squire. Another who was drawn into the conspiracy was Antonio Enriquez, a page of Pérez, who was to play the important part of mixing the poison into Escobedo's wine.

The poison was put into the wine as planned, but either it lacked the expected potency or Escobedo was able to throw off the effects, for the next day he was as well as he had ever been.

Again he was invited to dine, and again he was given the poison. This time he was very ill. An attempt to finish what had been begun was carried out by an accomplice in Escobedo's own kitchens, and more poison was put into the soup. Escobedo however took one sip and, tasting something strange, grew suspicious; he called one of his dogs to him, gave him the soup and shortly afterwards his fears were confirmed by the death of the dog. One of his slaves was hanged on suspicion.

Meanwhile, according to the most popular – and most likely – version of this story, Escobedo discovered the relationship between Pérez and the Princess of Éboli. He had been so devoted to Ruy Gómez that he was very shocked, and he threatened to tell the King of the intrigue between the pair.

There was a reason why the thought of Philip's hearing of the intrigue alarmed both the Princess and Antonio Pérez. The

King had been a great friend of the Ébolis and many people believed that he was the lover of the Princess; some say that he aspired to make her his mistress and failed. Others state that Ruy Gómez had been a complaisant husband and had even arranged the love affair between the King and his wife in order to retain his influence at Court. It has even been said that the King confided in Antonio Pérez regarding his unrequited passion for the Princess at that time when Pérez was her successful lover.

Whichever version is true, there is no doubt that Philip had a great interest in the Princess and that, when Escobedo threatened to tell the King what he had discovered, she and Antonio Pérez decided that Escobedo must die without delay.

Poison was unreliable, so Pérez sent his page, Antonio Enriquez, to Catalonia for a special kind of dagger, and it was arranged that Escobedo should be waylaid in the streets of Madrid by a band of assassins when Miguel, brother of Antonio Enriquez, should strike the fatal blow. The steward, Diego Martinez, brought in two assassins from Aragon, and added to these was Gil de Mesa, a devotee of Pérez, and two others.

It is difficult to understand why it should have been necessary to call in so many to accomplish one murder; and it seems that in doing so, Pérez was being unnecessarily reckless. It may have been that having made more than one unsuccessful attempt he was going to be certain that should one man fail to strike the fatal blow, others would be on hand to do so. However, the fact remains that on 31st March, 1578, Escobedo was killed in a street of Madrid.

It was not long before there were rumours that Pérez had instigated the murder, and Mateo Vázquez, a fellow secretary of Pérez, who was jealous of the latter's influence with Philip and determined to oust him from his favoured position, went to Philip and told him of these rumours.

The Princess, when she heard what Mateo Vázquez had done, could not restrain her fury, and she declared that the interfering secretary should share the fate of Escobedo. This did not help matters, and Philip, who preferred to work in the dark, was growing very uneasy.

He must tread warily, for it was on his orders that Pérez had arranged for Escobedo's murder; but if he had been deceived and Escobedo was removed, not because of his intrigues with Don John, but because he had threatened to carry to the King tales of the intrigue between Pérez and the Princess, this was a very different matter. Such deceit, such profligacy, roused Philip's cold and implacable anger.

At the end of the year Don John died suddenly in camp near Namur. He is said to have died of spotted fever, though many believed that a dose of poison had carried him off. He was very young; he had been full of vigour; it was true that disappointments in Flanders had depressed him; but was such depression enough to carry off a healthy young man? The general verdict is that he died of the fever, which would not be difficult to contract while in camp. But his death did follow suspiciously close on that of Escobedo, and with it were removed Philip's fears of one who might have become a rival.

Meanwhile Escobedo's wife implored the King to bring her husband's murderer to justice; and Philip, who after all had commanded that the murder should take place, falsely promised her that justice should be done.

The Princess of Éboli, now growing terrified of the rumours concerning herself and Pérez, which she knew must have reached the King, herself begged an audience of Philip. Philip's answer to her was characteristic of him; he assured the Princess, for whom he had once had such a great affection, that he would never forsake her (adding ominously) as long as she deserved his protection.

Philip had to act and there can be no doubt that after months of hesitancy he decided to sacrifice Pérez. First he had to replace him, and he recalled Cardinal Granvelle who was living in retirement in Rome. Granvelle reached the Escorial on 29th July, 1579, and as soon as Philip knew that the Cardinal was at hand he ordered the arrest of Pérez and the Princess of Éboli.

The Princess was imprisoned for nearly two years, after which she was allowed to return to Pastrana; but she was not permitted to live in freedom and was again taken to a prison where she remained until she died in 1592 – the punishment for having deceived and humiliated Philip II of Spain.

With Pérez under restraint it was important to Philip to

retrieve those papers which would incriminate him in the murder of Escobedo and which he knew must be among the secretary's possessions. At this point Juana de Coello, wife of Pérez, began to show the stuff of which she was made. Realizing that, if she gave up the documents and they were destroyed, her husband could be convicted of murder for his own ends, she stubbornly refused to relinquish them, even when threatened with imprisonment and starvation. Pérez, however, hearing of her plight, wrote to her ordering her to deliver up the papers; he had, with accustomed astuteness, provided for this situation and had already extracted those documents which incriminated the King, and had deposited them in a secret place.

As in all such situations which arose in Spain, time seemed unimportant. The Princess and Pérez continued in prison while Philip was making up his mind how he should act. Ten years after the arrest the friends of Pérez raised twenty thousand ducats which the Escobedo family agreed to accept in return for calling off the case for the prosecution. But Philip did not easily forget and, while prepared to wait for many years, he was determined to have his revenge in the end.

In February 1590, Pérez was put on the rack and at the eighth turn of the *cordeles* he confessed that he had arranged the murder of Escobedo, but that he had done so at the order of the King.

After the torture Antonio Pérez was so ill that his wife was allowed to visit him. This courageous woman arranged an escape (knowing that by doing so she would place herself in the utmost jeopardy) and Pérez was enabled to reach Aragon. He had a special reason for this: he was Aragonese, and the old law of Aragon was that the Court of Justicia could protect its oppressed people against the King himself, if the need arose.

The time was propitious because Aragon was insisting that its Viceroy should be of Aragonese descent, and Philip was contesting this.

Philip, made furious by the escape of Pérez and the part his wife had played in it, ordered that Juana and her children be immediately arrested. This was done and they were sent to prison where they remained for nine years – until after the death of Philip. Nor was he going to allow Pérez to elude him.

He gave orders that he should be brought back to Castile.

Taking no chances Pérez made with all speed to the Convent of St Peter's at Calatayud where he placed himself in sanctuary. Pérez had been accompanied in his escape by Gil de Mesa, who was to prove a faithful friend to the end of his life. It was Gil de Mesa who, in the disguise of a groom, had had horses waiting for him when he had escaped from his prison. Now realizing that Philip's men would have little respect for the sanctuary of the convent, Gil de Mesa went with all speed to Saragossa, where he claimed for Pérez, the *manifestacion* which would assure him of the protection of the Justicia of Aragon even though the King himself came against him.

Since the Aragonese were at this time determined to cling to their independence, Gil de Mesa was successful in his appeal, and many of the noblemen and officials arrived at the convent in order to escort Pérez to Saragossa, and lodge him in the prison there, the *cárcel de los manifestados,* for his own safety.

Prisoners who were taken there were not under the immediate authority of the King but were judged by the Chief Justice of Aragon. They could not be tortured or taken from the prison except after a fair trial in public court. This was one of their ancient privileges to which the Aragonese were determined to cling.

Philip, cautious as ever, now hesitated once more. He openly accused Pérez not only of the murder but of forging state documents and revealing state secrets. Pérez replied that he had documents in his possession which could prove that he had acted on orders from the King, and Philip temporarily abandoned the prosecution.

Philip, could see that, owing to the cunning of Pérez and conditions in Aragon, if he were not careful the man would escape him, and it was at this juncture that the King, realizing that Pérez while at large could betray many secrets, decided to call in the Inquisition. Had he been accustomed to using the Inquisition for political means he would have called in this most powerful of all instruments much earlier in the case; but it can be clearly seen that it was only when he found it impossible to proceed with the case by any other means that he decided to make use of it.

It was now necessary to bring a charge of heresy against Pérez, which was not easy, for Pérez was by no means a religious man and therefore he had never acted in any way which could be called other than orthodox.

The Count of Almenara, who had been sent to Aragon by Philip to deal with the differences between the Justicia and the sovereign, was put in charge of the case and told to find the necessary evidence to bring Pérez to the notice of the Inquisition.

Almenara bribed Diego Bustamente, an old servant of Pérez, who then declared that he had heard his master blaspheme, for he had said that if God slept during his trial and did not perform a miracle in his favour he would lose his faith. He was reported as saying that if God the Father put any obstacle in his way he would cut off His nose.

These words were clearly spoken with the utmost lightness but the Inquisitors worked hard on them and the result was that they were declared blasphemous, scandalous and impious and, inasmuch as Pérez had declared his belief that God had a body, they were heretical.

The *alguazils* and all the dreaded officials of the Holy Office were sent to make the arrest; but the jailer refused to hand over his prisoner even to the Inquisition unless he had permission from the Justicia to do so. The officials of the Inquisition were forced to leave; they wrote to the jailer threatening him with excommunication and a fine of a thousand ducats for daring to obstruct the Inquisition. The jailer merely sent this communication to the Chief Justice, Juan de la Naza, who, seeing that the order came from the dreaded Holy Office, decided to take the safe course and obey. Pérez was then conducted to the prison of the Inquisition.

Pérez however, aware of what was happening, had already sent word to his friends in Aragon. The Inquisition was resented there and its high-handed action in taking a man from their prison could be construed as a deliberate slight and insult to an old custom. The friends of Pérez went into the streets, crying out that the liberty of Aragon was at stake; and men poured out of the houses and marched to Almenara's house, because they felt that he, who was in Aragon on the Kings' business, was at the root of this attempt to curtail their liberty.

Almenara was attacked and, although he was rescued from the mob, he died of his wounds two weeks after the incident.

While one section of the mob was attacking Almenara, another was marching to the Aljafería, the old Moorish castle, which was the headquarters of the Inquisition. They threatened to set fire to the place and would have done so if the Inquisitors, knowing themselves worsted, had not agreed to hand over Pérez. He was then taken in triumph back to his old quarters.

Pérez was too wise to feel complacent; he knew that the people of Aragon could not stand out against the forces of the King which would surely be sent to subdue them; he knew that if he remained in Spain the Inquisition would in time make him its prisoner.

He procured a file with which he worked on the bars of his window, and was ready for escape one dark night, but was betrayed by Juan de Besante whom he had believed he could trust. He was in despair, knowing full well what his fate would be at the hands of the Holy Office.

Arrangements were made to remove him, and the *alguazils*, with all the officials of the Inquisition who, determined not to be foiled again, brought with them a band of three thousand armed men, came to the prison to take him.

The carriage which was to take Pérez to the dungeons of the Aljafería was waiting and he was about to be fettered, when a crowd of rioters led by that most faithful of friends, Gil de Mesa, arrived and shouting slogans about the liberty of Aragon, stormed into the prison, pushed aside the Inquisitors and set them running for their lives, while Pérez was seized and carried to a near-by house where horses were waiting. He made his way to Saragossa and there attempted to cross the frontier, but this was heavily guarded and he was forced to hide in the house of a friend until plans could be made for him to leave the country.

Philip meanwhile had despatched an army under Alphonso de Vargas to punish the rebellious Aragonese. Philip, shrewd statesman that he was, recognized the opportunity this affair had given him of suppressing the old customs of Aragon which limited the sovereign's power. He was also determined to impress on these people that it was a grave offence to show opposition to the Holy Office.

Pérez seems to have had a charmed life for he was given refuge in Navarre by Catherine, Princess of Béarn, sister of the King of France, Henri IV. When Philip's men arrived in Béarn and asked that the prisoner should be handed to them, Catherine refused to relinquish him, and, since Philip had no wish for trouble with Navarre, he was not inclined to resort to force.

During his stay in Barn, Pérez published two accounts of his own life which further angered the King; and many attempts were made to lure him back to Spain. But Pérez was fully aware of what his fate would be if he were such a fool as to return; and from Béarn he went to England where he was made much of by Philip's greatest enemy, Elizabeth I of England. After England he visited Paris and although attempts were made on his life he continued to survive. Philip died before he did, and although he knew that Philip's son, Philip III, would have allowed him to return to his native land in peace, Pérez believed that the Spanish Inquisition would never forget or forgive one who had flouted it.

Nevertheless in 1611 he was persuaded by the Bishop of the Canaries, who was General of the Franciscans, that if he were to return to Spain and offer himself to the Inquisition, after a mock trial he would be given his liberty. Pérez, tired of the wandering life, nostalgic and longing now to see his children and the wife who had done so much for him, wrote to the Bishop and told him that as soon as his safe-conduct arrived he would leave for Spain.

He sent to his wife a petition, in which he described his sufferings, and asked her to pass it to the Supreme Council. This she did; but perhaps because the Inquisition moved ponderously as it ever did, Pérez died before the safe-conduct was given him.

He had spent twenty years banished from his country.

His case is notable not because it resembles a romantic adventure story but because of its effect on the history of Aragon.

The Justicia, who had been in office only three months and who was but twenty-seven years old, was publicly beheaded as a result of the rising, and at an *auto de fé* on 29th April, 1592, many of those who had taken leading parts in the disturbances appeared. Six of these people were released and the rest sentenced either to exile from Aragon or to the galleys.

Philip had taken an oath that the constitution of Aragon should be respected, and he dared not openly break his word; but the Aragonese had seen Philip's soldiers in their towns, they had seen the power of the Inquisition extended, and they knew that they would be most unwise to show opposition to the will of the King.

Another occasion when Philip used the Inquisition for political ends was in the case of Jeanne of Navarre. He commanded that the Inquisition should prepare a case against her – no difficult matter since Jeanne was an ardent Huguenot – and that she should be captured and brought before the tribunal of Saragossa. Had this been effected, Jeanne would undoubtedly have been burned at the stake as a heretic; which would have been very advantageous to Philip's designs on Navarre.

The account of Philip's invoking the Inquisition in the case of his son, Don Carlos, is not so reliable; and the death of the young Prince is wrapped in mystery.

If he were murdered by his father, it is very possible that Philip did instruct Inquisitor-General Espinosa to prepare a case against him. It would be in keeping with Philip's character to find an adequate excuse for the removal of a son whose existence was becoming intolerable to him, and who, in the opinion of Catholic Spain, deserved death more than a heretic.

Wild, stormy Carlos had been a source of trouble not only to his father but to all those about him for many years. Philip, sternly devoted to duty, must have suffered great anxieties when he thought of his crown's passing to such a man. Carlos had already attacked Cardinal Espinosa (the Inquisitor-General) because he had banished from Madrid an actor whom Carlos favoured. The attacks of Carlos were always violent, and he had drawn his sword and would have killed Espinosa had he not been prevented in time. 'A little priest to dare oppose me!' he is reputed to have said. If Philip did call in Espinosa to prepare a case of heresy against his son, there can be little doubt that the Cardinal would have gone to work with a will.

Carlos had greatly desired to go to the Netherlands as Governor, and had openly shown his sympathy with the Flemings. He put forward schemes for pacifying these people which may have shown the Inquisition that if ever he came to the throne there would be stormy times ahead. When he heard that Alva was to be sent he tried to stab him.

Carlos was obviously tottering on the edge of madness. His hatred for his father grew to such an extent that he made no effort to hide it. The fact that Philip had married Elisabeth of France, the daughter of Henri Deux and Catherine de'Medici, inflamed that hatred, for Elisabeth had at one time been promised to Carlos. When the beautiful young Princess arrived in Spain, Carlos is said to have fallen in love with her; and naturally many scandalous stories were circulated about them.

But it was when the foolish young man planned to murder his father, and confessed to his prior what he was about to, that the climax was reached.

How could Philip allow this madman to reach the throne? Carlos was arrested and kept a prisoner, and Philip is reputed to have said that the reason for his imprisonment was not his misconduct or lack of respect towards his father, but that the measure rested upon another foundation and must be adopted in order that Philip might satisfy his obligations to God and the people. This would seem as though the theory that Carlos was arrested on account of his heresy might be true.

Also Pius V, after reading a letter from Philip concerning the arrest of Carlos, is said to have remarked to the Spanish Ambassador that the preservation of Christian Spain was dependent upon Philip's living for many years and having a successor who would tread in his footsteps. Philip's words to Carlos de Seso at the Valladolid *auto de fé* will be remembered. When de Seso asked him how he could endure to see his subjects so persecuted, he answered that he would carry the faggots for his own son if he were a heretic.

Those who support this theory say that that trial would naturally have been conducted in secrecy and the Prince could have been condemned to death. It is understandable that the heir to the throne could not take part in an *auto de fé*; therefore it was decided to poison him.

He died at the age of twenty-three and, although it was given out that quartan fever was the cause of death, most contemporary writers attributed it to poison.

De Thou states that Carlos was condemned by the Inquisitors and that subsequently poison was put into his broth. Others also assert that he was condemned by the Inquisition and poisoned.

We cannot be sure but, if the Inquisition did try Carlos and condemn him, this would be a case of the Inquisition's being used for political purposes, for there was no doubt that it was politically important to keep Carlos from inheriting the throne.

## CHAPTER FOUR

# THE MOORISH TRAGEDY

Philip died in September 1598 after a long and painful illness, and was succeeded by his son, Philip III. Although the power of the great Spanish Empire was beginning to crack, Philip II had succeeded in making Spain even more uniformly Catholic than it had been during the reign of his father.

Philip III was lazy and good tempered, the kind of king who was almost certain to be easily swayed by his favourites; and it was during his reign that there took place that event which was to prove so calamitous to the prosperity of Spain: the expulsion of the Moors.

When Philip II inherited the crown the exchequer was in a sadly depleted condition. Trade had been adversely affected by the *alcabala*, that tax which was levied on sales and purchases; and it was realized that the people could not be made to pay what they did not possess.

The third Philip was not a prudent man as his father had been; Philip II had lived like a hermit, had dressed in sombre fashion and had eschewed ostentation of any sort; not so his son. Philip III loved magnificence and when he travelled through the countryside to meet his bride, in spite of the country's poverty, the splendour of his equipage was compared with the brilliant displays which had been seen in the days of the Emperor.

The bride was Margaret of Austria, and before his death Philip II had also arranged a marriage between his daughter Isabella and the Archduke Albert. Margaret and Albert had travelled through Italy with the utmost magnificence, and the marriages had been celebrated by proxy at Ferrara by Clement VIII.

After his marriage Philip and Margaret travelled to Aragon where he, in his easy-going way, granted amnesty to those prisoners who had been arrested during the recent risings in Aragon. The people of Aragon, who had been so crushed and had seen the soldiers in their towns and the Inquisition more powerful than ever, were enthusiastic in their welcome of the new king. They ventured to ask Philip to abolish the Inquisition, but even Philip realized that he could not go as far as that, and his answer to that request was very evasive.

The position of the Moriscos was becoming more and more precarious. It had been decreed that however slight the suspicion of heresy they incurred, it should be treated as vehement and even if there was but a single witness against them, they must be sent to the galleys for three years or more, whereas in the case of victims who were not Moriscos, if the evidence against them was given by a single witness, they had a slight chance of acquittal and a very good one of having the examination suspended.

Moriscos who did not confess under torture and could not therefore be condemned to the stake were nevertheless punished with whipping and fines.

In the year 1594, of ninety-six Moriscos who underwent torture, fifty-three came through without confessing. This was a great number and might imply that the Moriscos were capable of suffering in silence; but there are suggestions that some torturers would, providing the bribe offered was large enough, modify the torment. In 1604 a torturer was brought to trial for accepting bribes from Moriscos. This may have had something to do with the ability of many Moriscos to endure the torture.

The Archbishop of Ribera was eager that the Moriscos should be expelled from Spain, as it was impossible to kill them all. They were becoming the most persecuted sect in Spain and, according to a Toledo record from 1575 to 1610, while there were one hundred and seventy-four Marranos and forty-seven Protestants among the victims of the Inquisition, there were one hundred and ninety Moriscos.

In 1563 Guerrero, Archbishop of Granada, had visited Pius IV whom he told that his flock in Granada called themselves Christians but were such in name only; and later, on returning to Spain, he begged Philip to rid Spain of Moriscos. Philip sent Guerrero's complaint to a special council of the Inquisition,

59

and it was decided that the Moors must be forced to be Christians in fact. The old edict of 1526 was revived. The people were forbidden to speak or write Arabic; the doors of the houses were to be kept open during feast-days and marriages, as well as on Fridays; the use of henna was forbidden; baths, public and private, were to be destroyed, and so on.

These rules were accepted with a very bad grace by the Moors; and when it was learned that children between the ages of three and fifteen were to be taken from their parents to be brought up in the Christian Faith and to speak Castilian, the anxiety among the Moorish population grew fast; for although the Moors looked on with apprehension while their precious baths were destroyed they were more than angry at the prospect of losing their children.

In spite of the fact that they would be pitting their small strength against the might of Spain, the Moors prepared to fight for their freedom. They believed they could raise a hundred thousand men and that they would be supported by their kinsmen of Africa.

A rising was planned for Holy Thursday, 18th April, 1568, but their intention was betrayed so that it was necessary to postpone the date; and it was not until 23rd December that it took place.

Captain-General Mondéjar, a grandson of Count Tendilla, who had been put in charge of Granada by Isabella and Ferdinand at the time of the Re-conquest, had constantly warned Philip and the Inquisitor-General Espinosa that the revolt planned by the Moriscos would be on a large scale, and he had asked for reinforcements. Espinosa refused to recognize his need and thus, when the revolt came Mondéjar was not very well prepared to combat it.

Yet he dealt vigorously with the insurgents and by February he had crushed the revolt; but those who were clamouring for the extinction of the Moors saw here a chance to accomplish this. Granada was not easily subdued, and the Moors, no doubt feeling their position to be desperate indeed, set up their standard in the mountains of the Alpujarras and in a short time the entire kingdom of Granada was ready for war.

Philip appointed his bastard half-brother Don John to command the army. Don John was then little more than a boy and his experience was not great.

This war was carried on with the utmost cruelty. Men were massacred by the thousand, and the women and children captured that they might be sold as slaves. It is said that the soldiers set out their expeditions, not to fight a battle, but to hunt for slaves. These soldiers, not content with wreaking their inhumanity upon the Moors, even attacked the villages through which they passed, robbing and murdering as they went.

After the battle of Galera two thousand Moors were discovered, huddled together in a square; they cried out for mercy as Don John's men approached, but these Christian warriors knew no mercy. The Moors were shot in spite of their entreaties; and four hundred women and children who were discovered in the town were treated in the same way. Don John had ordered that not a living soul in Galera should be spared, because the Spaniards had suffered more loss than he had anticipated in the town's capture.

For this gallant exploit the Pope hailed Don John as the Champion of Christendom. Philip was pleased and gave thanks to Our Lady of Guadaloupe for the glorious victory.

Pedro de Deza, who was a member of the Suprema and had been appointed president of the Chancellory of Granada, now desired to move the population of Granada to the mountains in the north of Spain.

This plan was to be put into practice in 1569. The men were divided into groups, their hands tied with ropes, and marched off under guard. The women were allowed to remain for a while that they might first sell what they could of their household goods. On the road to the north many died of starvation; many were killed by robbers; and others were taken to be sold as slaves.

This method was applied to town after town as they fell into the hands of the Spaniards.

The suffering of the Moors was so great that it wrung pity from Don John who wrote to Ruy Gómez that many Moorish families who had been deported from the district of Guadix had met on the road such a blizzard that members of families had lost each other; and that it was difficult to imagine anything more to be pitied than the depopulation of a kingdom.

Strangely even the Moors, like the Jews, as soon as they were allowed to settle in any place began to prosper. Whereas the Jews had possessed a financial wizardry, the Moors by their energetic labour, in particular on the land, began to cast off their poverty. Again as with the Jews it may have been that the hatred of the people towards the race was based more on envy of their prosperity than on the differences in their religions.

It was feared that within a few years these people who had been robbed of their privileges and allowed, as a great concession, to settle in certain districts, would soon by their industry make themselves masters of the land and employ those very natives who had graciously consented to receive them as an inferior people. Complaints were put forward that they never went to war, that they did not enter the church but were devoted solely to their work; and, because they were prepared to work harder for less wages than the Spaniards, employers of labour preferred them to the latter.

The character of the Moors can be assessed when it is considered that they were able to grow to prosperity in spite of the rigorous laws against them: they were to be flogged if they left the districts to which they had been sent, and not only flogged but sent for a term to the galleys; they were forbidden to observe their Moorish customs and there were harsh penalties for possessing Arabic books; yet this industrious people, in spite of these restrictions, began to rise to prosperity.

It is inconceivable that the laws imposed upon them should always have been obeyed; and there must have been a smouldering resentment against the people who had treated them so badly. Certain Moriscos became bandits; others, who had become rich, offered Philip a bribe of thirty thousand ducats if he would allow them to carry arms. Philip, considering the state of the treasury, was unable to resist this offer and, in a certain district the Moors soon began to live much as they pleased, and if any of their number were caught and brought for trial, there were irresistible bribes waiting for their accusers.

In 1608 the Moriscos of Valencia were in touch with Muley Cidan, who was a pretender to the throne of Morocco. They promised him two hundred thousand men if he would bring twenty thousand to Spain and join with them against the Spaniards.

When this plot was discovered it filled the King, Philip III, and his Court with alarm and schemes were put forward for ridding Spain of the troublesome Moors.

The fact that Muley Cidan did not wish to be embroiled in the troubles of the Moors in Spain did not prevent the King and his counsellors from continuing to think of ridding the country of the Moors. They had become a menace. They plotted with the corsairs of Barbary and when Henri Quatre was planning an attack on Spain he believed with reason that he could rely on the help of the Moors.

In 1609 it was decided to banish all Moors from Spain beginning with the troublesome district of Valencia, and in August of that year Don Agustin de Mexia was sent to Valencia to carry out the expulsion. Ribera, who had been one of the chief agitators for the expulsion, had realized what disaster would be wrought in the districts of Aragon and Valencia if the Moors were driven out; he had at last understood that where the Moors were allowed to continue with their industrious lives there was prosperity, and although he wished to expel them from other parts of Spain he desired to keep them in his own districts of Valencia and Aragon where, he maintained, they could be controlled. Therefore when Agustin de Mexia arrived in Valencia, Ribera suggested that he should join with him and put it to the King that Valencia and Aragon be left in peace and the expulsion begin in Andalusia.

This appeal was ignored and by September sixty-two galleys and fourteen galleons brought some eight thousand troops to the area.

The order was given that the Moors were to confine themselves to their houses for three days to await instructions; anyone failing to do so would suffer death. They were then ordered to leave at once for the port to which they were directed. They were allowed to take with them as much as they could carry and their destination was Barbary.

The Spanish inhabitants of the area made immediate protest, for how, they demanded, were the sugar and rice crops to be saved if all the workers were deported. Who was going to irrigate the canals, a task which the Moors had always so expertly handled? It was necessary even for the most fanatical to consider this problem, and eventually it was decided that six per cent of the Moriscos should be allowed to remain.

Those to stay were selected in this way: Those who for two years had observed no Moorish customs; all children of under four, and children under six whose fathers were Old Christians, might stay with their father, and if the mother was a Morisco she might stay also; but if the father was a Morisco he must go, and if the mother was an Old Christian she was to stay and keep the children with her.

This splitting of families produced great anguish, and it was immediately necessary to bring in a stern penalty for giving shelter to those who had been ordered to go: six years in the galleys.

The Moors, who had at first been resentful and ready to do battle, suddenly seemed to understand that there was no hope in resisting. They decided that they would all go – even the selected six per cent who, although they had been offering bribes to be allowed to stay, were soon being offered bribes by the other side to stay.

The only bribe they would accept was freedom to follow their own religion. So desperate was one owner of a sugar plantation – the Duke of Gandía – that he went so far as to ask if this concession could be granted. The answer was that even the King had no power to allow such a concession; so the Duke, in desperation, was forced to contemplate the ruin of his sugar crop. There were many others in the district who were in a similar position.

This was a case of history's repeating itself; in this instance the Moors were playing the tragic role which more than a hundred years before had been taken by the Jews. They were selling their rich possessions and getting scarcely anything for them, just as years before the Jews had bartered a vineyard for a piece of cloth.

When the first shock was over some of the Moors did not

64

seem heart-broken at the prospect of leaving Spain. No doubt they thought of the Inquisition which had continually threatened their lives, and dreamed of following their own religion openly; moreover they were an industrious people and they knew that wherever they were able to settle they would soon begin to prosper.

But there were some who resisted. Between fifteen and twenty-five thousand of them could not bear to leave the land where their ancestors had lived for so many centuries, and they sought refuge in the mountains. They were not allowed to remain in their sanctuary, but were rounded up and thousands of them massacred; the remnant, suffering from starvation, offered themselves up to the authorities for transportation to Africa. Few of them reached the ports, for the barbarous soldiers robbed and murdered most of the men and took the women and children to sell as slaves.

While the Moors of Valencia were being expelled, preparations for exodus were taking place in other districts. Aragon, Catalonia, Murcia and Val de Ricote followed, until in 1615 the plan for deportation had been completely carried out.

It is impossible to say how many people were driven from their homes in this great exodus. Records vary from 300,000 to 3,000,000. Llorente suggests 1,000,000, but many statisticians have declared this to be exaggerated. The fact remains that many thousands suffered; and for the purpose of creating an all-Catholic Spain, that country, determined to destroy its prosperity, drove from its borders a very valuable section of its population. The rich agricultural country became as a desert; the system of irrigation was neglected so that where there had been prosperous farms there were ruined farmhouses and infertile land.

The Inquisition had however lost one rich source of victims, although naturally Moriscos appeared now and then in the *auto de fé*. Many people had retained their Moorish slaves of whom, owing to the custom of selling captured people into slavery, there were many.

As late as May 1728 forty-five Moors appeared in an *auto*; and in October of that year there were another twenty-eight. In 1769 the Inquisition discovered that a mosque had been set up by Moors who secretly worshipped there. But from 1780 to 1820 there is no case of a Morisco's being brought before the tribunal of the Holy Office. (Lea, from the *Archives of Valencia*.)

Thus the Inquisition was triumphant. It had rid the country of a race which, having been forced to baptism, was likely to lapse into heresy. Bigotry was once more served at the expense of reason.

## CHAPTER FIVE

# THE INQUISITION IN MEXICO

When Isabella had financed voyages of discovery she had proclaimed – and believed this to be so – that her motive in doing so was to spread the Catholic Faith all over the world; and there can be no doubt that Philip II shared his great-grandmother's sentiments in this respect, although many of the adventurers who set out on these voyages appeared to be more interested in the richness of the booty to be won than in the saving of souls.

As was to be expected, among those who set out from Spain to populate the new world were many Jews who, despairing of ever being able to live in peace in Spain, sought refuge elsewhere. There was an effort to prevent Jews from sharing in these ventures, but Ferdinand was always open to bribes, and a law was made that for a price – twenty thousand ducats – any merchant could go to the colonies and trade there for two years. Emperor Charles repealed the law, but after some negotiations it was revived – and the price was raised to eighty thousand ducats.

Before the Inquisition was set up in the Spanish possessions a very costly method of bringing heretics to trial was practised. The case of Pedro de Leon, which occurred in 1515, gives a good illustration of this. Pedro with his family had gone to Hispañola where they hoped to live in peace beyond the shadow of the Holy Office. They were mistaken, for the Inquisitor-General of Seville sent one of his officials to bring them back to Spain. Orders were given that a ship was to be provided for this purpose, and any other escaping heretics were to be returned at the same time. How much less costly and how much simpler it would be to have the Inquisitors on the spot!

The Emperor Charles was very much aware of this, and in 1519 Cardinal Adrian was appointed Inquisitor-General of the

Indies with the Bishop of Puerto Rico, Alfonso Manso, and Pedro de Cordova, a Dominican monk, as Inquisitors.

These were followed by Martin de Valencia who went to Mexico with a dozen men of the Franciscan Order to which he belonged. Others followed, but little is known of their activities until the century had grown old, and then we hear of Lutherans being burned and suffering lighter penances, and a woman's being reconciled to the Church after having made a pact with the Devil.

There is an account (Lea, *Inquisition in the Spanish Dependencies*) of a Flemish painter, Simon Pereyns, who, in conversation with a fellow artist, happened to state that fornication was not a sin; his friend argued with him about this but Pereyns persisted in defending his assertion.

But later, on sober consideration, he considered it prudent to present himself to the tribunal and confess what he had said, for he believed that by reporting himself he would attract less suspicion than if someone denounced him. Moreover it was frequently said that sexual intercourse between the unmarried was no sin, and in Spain at this time the Inquisition was attempting to correct this popular belief. In 1559 at an *auto de fé* in Seville there were twelve cases of people who had made this same statement; some suffered whippings and others were sentenced to parade in the *vergüenza* (public whipping through the streets, stripped to the waist).

Later, in 1562, there were twenty-five such cases, all forced to appear at the *auto* wearing nothing but shirts, and carrying candles; some were beaten, others heavily fined; and most of them were gagged, presumably to remind them that they should have kept their mouths shut.

Even as late as 1818 there is an account of one lieutenant accusing another before the Valencia tribunal of saying there was no sin in fornication.

Simon Pereyns no doubt thought that he would escape with a light reprimand, but he was mistaken. He was put into prison and, when the artist to whom he had stated his views was questioned, he remembered that Pereyns had said that he found the painting of portraits more interesting as well as more profitable than painting holy images. This was considered as a remark tinged with heresy, and Pereyns was tortured. He was put on the rack and given three turns of the *cordeles*, and in addition was made to suffer the water torture to the extent of three jars.

He endured all this without confessing to heresy, but he was not given his freedom. Instead he was called upon to pay the cost of his trial and to paint an altar piece for the church, which should be a picture of Our Lady of Merced.

Those who stood in judgment in Mexico at that time were not officials of the Holy Office but merely ecclesiastical courts which must submit any extraordinary evidence to Spain to be considered by the Holy Office there.

It was in January of 1569 that it was arranged to set up the Inquisition proper in the Spanish Dependencies, and as this matter proceeded in the usual dilatory way it was not until a year later, 3rd January, 1570, that Doctor Moya de Contreras was informed by Espinosa that he had been selected as Inquisitor-General for Mexico.

To be banished from Spain on such a mission might not seem very agreeable, and Moya de Contreras (who at first declined to accept the post) was told that it was to be only of short duration and that for his services he would be awarded the Archbishopric of Mexico. He was more or less forced to accept, and it became the custom, when appointing his successors, to indicate that some great honour would be given after a few years' service in Mexico – a necessary inducement.

Contreras did not reach Mexico City until September 1571; and when he did so ceremonies and spectacles were arranged that the population might realize the importance of what was happening.

Contreras was conducted to the church with great pomp and after the sermon, letters from Philip II were read aloud to the crowds assembled, explaining the dangers of heresy and that the Inquisitors had come to Mexico in order to prevent the spread of this evil, and how all who were discovered to be concerned in its growth would be brought before the Inquisition to answer for their sins.

An Edict of Faith was then read, accompanied by the usual threats and promises, and all present were commanded to raise their right hands and swear to accept and obey the Inquisition.

The Edict of Faith soon began to have the desired effect, and the prisons were filled with those suspected of heresy. Contreras appointed an *alguazil*-mayor of the city, a receiver of confiscations, an *alcaide* of the secret prison and other officials.

The first Mexican *auto de fé* was held on 28th February, 1574, and was performed with as much solemnity as though it were taking place in one of the large Spanish towns. Two weeks before the fixed date, drummers and trumpeters paraded the city and the announcements were made. People crowded into the city from the outlying neighbourhood and we are told that there were some seventy or eighty victims – thirty-six of whom were Lutherans, mostly English sailors.

Contreras retired from his position in 1573, for the promise to make him Archbishop of Mexico was kept; and he was followed by Bonilla who in turn became Archbishop of Mexico on Contreras's return to Spain, and Bonilla was followed by Alonso Granero de Avalos.

An incident concerning Granero gives a clear illustration of his character and indicates the fear which must have haunted all who came into contact with the Inquisitors.

Granero was in the habit of selecting people at random and fining them in order to pay his expenses; and when a notary, Rodrigo de Evora, wrote some verses, stressing the habits of the Inquisitor-General, which fell into his possession, the unlucky man was arrested on Granero's orders and put into prison.

His feet and hands were chained and he was afterwards put on the rack where he was so severely treated that his joints were dislocated. He was then condemned to appear at an *auto de fé* where his punishment was proclaimed to be three hundred lashes and six years in the galleys. His property was confiscated by Granero who kept it for himself.

This was one of the men who were charged with the spiritual guidance of Mexico.

One of the most cruel of the Inquisitors was Alonso de Peralta who took office in 1594; no sooner had he arrived in Mexico that the activity of the Inquisition increased; *autos de fé* took place more frequently, and more people were condemned to be burned. One victim, Luis de Carvajal, said that he hoped he would not have to look on Peralta's face, for the mere sight of him 'made his flesh creep'. (Lea's *The Inquisition in the Spanish Dependencies* from Adler.)

This Luis de Carvajal was a man of some position and his crime was that he had not denounced his sisters who had been found guilty of heresy. For this he was robbed of his offices and later tortured and burned in the *auto* of 1596.

The best way to understand how the Inquisition worked in Mexico is to look at some of the recorded cases, and one of the most interesting is that of an Irishman, William Lamport or Guillen Lombardo de Guzman. He aroused the interest of the Inquisition when he made a startling claim. At the time Philip IV was on the throne, and Lamport said that although his mother was an Irish woman he was an illegitimate son of Philip III and therefore half-brother to the reigning king.

It was said of him that he planned a rising in Mexico in order that it might break away from Spain, and that in such an event Mexico's ruler should be the illegitimate son of Philip III.

The Inquisition had not arrested him on this charge however, but had not found it difficult to bring him to trial on one which was within its jurisdiction. In order to assure the success of his treasonable schemes, it was said, he had consulted sorcerers and astrologers; which was, of course, a crime against the Church.

Whether or not Lamport was the son of Philip III is not known, but the account he gave of his life appeared to have verisimilitude. He said that he had been born in England where he lived for twelve years; young as he was he had written a pamphlet directed at the King, and for this reason had been forced to leave the country. He had adventures in various parts of the world and, so he said, had been received by Philip himself, who had given him the title of Marquis and instructions to take over the viceroyalty from the present Viceroy. The papers he showed, purporting to come from Philip, were discovered to be forged, but at the same time Lamport was very knowledgeable concerning the Court and, although he was put in prison – where he remained for seventeen years – orders came from the Suprema in Spain that he was to be treated with consideration and, if he wished it, to be given a companion to share his cell.

71

He was provided with one, and very soon he had induced the man to share in a very elaborate plan for escape. Like all Lamport's plans it was worked out in detail, and in theory seemed flawless. This plan might have worked, but it seems that during his long confinement Lamport's mind had become unbalanced and on the night fixed for the escape, instead of making off to some safe place, he lingered in the town posting his writings in prominent places and trying to persuade a man to take a letter to the viceroy in which he demanded the arrest of the Inquisitors.

Eventually, after hours had been wasted, he hid himself, for as it was now daylight he had little hope of getting far away; and he was very soon recaptured.

When he was put into a well-guarded cell and fettered, he asked for pen and paper and, in view of the orders that he should receive special treatment, these were given to him. He then wrote a vitriolic attack on the Inquisition, after which he was not allowed to have paper, so he wrote on the sheets of his bed.

As time passed he became more and more unbalanced in his mind, and in 1659 he was condemned to the flames for sorcery, heresy and plotting rebellion.

Because he had written against the Inquisition a special punishment was ordained for him, and he was conducted to the *auto de fé* with the painful gag in his mouth and, while his sentence was read, he was hung up by his right arm and thus hanging had to listen to his new sentence.

He was to have been burned alive but, as the flames were lighted, he threw himself against the iron ring about his throat with such repeated violence that he killed himself.

When the Suprema heard what had happened to him, and that the Mexican Inquisition had acted without orders from Spain, they were very angry. Why the Suprema should have been so concerned for the life of Lamport has never been discovered; but it makes one wonder whether there might have been a grain of truth in the story of his royal birth. (Lea, *The Inquisition in the Spanish Dependencies*.)

Among others who suffered at the same time as Lamport was

an old man named Sebastian Alvàrez who had declared he was Christ. For this he was condemned to be burned alive; when he reached the *quemadero* however he 'confessed' and was given the mercy of strangulation as the fires were lighted.

Francisco López de Aponte was, in the same *auto*, accused of sorcery as well as heresy. He was pronounced to be sane and therefore fit for punishment, and when he was cruelly tortured he bore his suffering with such fortitude that it appeared he was insensible to pain. It seemed certain, to his tormentors, that he was in league with the Devil who had given him this special power. Every part of his body was then shaved and a careful search made for the mark which would proclaim him a witch. He was again tortured and once more bore all that was inflicted with great calm; he was condemned to be burned alive. In his cell on the last night of his life he is reputed to have told the priest, who was urging him to become reconciled and so escape the hideous death by burning, that there was no God, no Heaven and no hell; there was only birth and death. He attended the *auto* in the same impassive state in which he had endured the torture, and without a groan stood still while the flames consumed his body.

Pedro García de Arias was a pedlar who had written three books, uneducated though he was, which were said to contain heresy. García had been whipped through the streets and was condemned to be burned at the stake. He declared that he had been misjudged but would not ask for mercy. But he changed his mind at the end when he saw the faggots about to be lighted. He was strangled before his body was burned; and the books which he had written were tied about his neck so that they might burn with his body. (Lea.)

Louis Ramé was a Frenchman who suffered at the hands of the Inquisition; and the Rev. J. Baker, M.A., in his collection of writings under the title of *The History of the Inquisition as it subsists in the Kingdoms of Spain etc. to this Day* gives what is purported to be Ramé's own account.

He was a sailor and had had a very adventurous life even before he fell into the hands of the Inquisition. He became captain of a cargo ship which carried wine and brandy from

Rochelle to Nantes and pilchards from Port Louis to Barcelona.

When war broke out between France and Holland he served for a while in the navy, and later, at Rochelle, married a widow with four children.

He could not spend his life at Rochelle however, and after three months he sailed for Fagal, Cayenne, and Martinico. Whilst on this voyage he was captured by a privateer who took his ship and set him ashore. He found a ship to carry him home, but this ship met disaster, sprung a leak and sank. Ramé and some others managed to scramble into a boat and drifted for five days, during which time they were without food or drink. They landed at Puerto Rico and after having feasted on oranges and water went in search of provisions for the boat. They found these, but the man who supplied them thought it necessary to warn the Governor of their presence and they were put under guard. They remained prisoners of the Governor for sixteen months.

Into the harbour came the Spanish ship *S. Lawrence*, and Ramé was taken aboard and carried to Vera Cruz. He was given a little money from the 'Charity Box which the King of Spain allows for poor Prisoners' and was told that he might go ashore and find work. He did this and became journeyman to a baker.

He did this work for some months, and then one night a Dutchman who lived in the baker's house became very ill, and a priest who visited him tried, while he was in a weak state, to make a Catholic of him. All the Dutchman could reply to the priest's earnest admonition to change his faith was that he did not understand.

The priest then remembered that there was a much-travelled Frenchman in the house who could probably speak the Dutchman's language; and Ramé was sent for and told to act as interpreter. This Ramé refused to do for, he said, he was himself a Protestant and would not allow the dying man, who was only half conscious of what was happening, to be perverted from his religion.

He was then told that *his* religion had been composed by 'ill persons and for to please libertines' and that the Pope was the Vicar of Jesus Christ.

'To which I answered [writes Ramé] that I had never heard our ministers preach anything else but the gospel, with strict orders to follow what our Saviour had commanded us, and that as to the Pope, I acknowledge him not as Vicar of Jesus Christ.'

This was courting danger, but on the 17th of December, 1678, Ramé committed an even more reckless action. He met the Holy Sacrament being carried through the streets, and refused to kneel to it.

He was arrested, taken as a prisoner to the house of a certain Don Pedro Estrada, and kept there on very small rations for two weeks with his feet fixed in stocks.

He was then put in irons and taken to the prison of the Inquisition and brought before the Inquisitors. Asked why he had not knelt to the Holy Sacrament, he said that he had read in the Holy Scriptures that idolatry was forbidden. He was then asked to abjure the Protestant Faith and on refusing was threatened with burning at the stake.

He was taken back to his cell and there he saw no one but his jailer, who said to him each morning and evening when he entered the cell: 'Praised be the Holy Sacrament of the Altar.' To this Ramé was obliged to answer or be accused of insolence, so he retaliated with: 'Praised be our Lord Jesus Christ,' or 'Praised be God.' The Fiscal, who Ramé tells us was 'a sort of Judge' visited him every Saturday for five months and tried to convert him to Catholicism.

Suddenly the food which was given him began to have a strange effect upon him. He was very ill and his mind wandered. After three months of this he was again brought before the tribunal, when he was accused of not paying the respect to the Sacrament which was due to it, and denying that the Pope was the Vicar of Jesus Christ; and when he was asked why he did not pray to the saints, he replied that Jesus had said: 'Come unto me all ye that are heavy laden and I shall give you rest.'

The Inquisitor, furious, cried out that he should be given the torture, ordinary and extraordinary, to which Ramé boldly answered that the torture they had already inflicted ought to satisfy them.

Back to his cell he was taken, to be visited every Saturday for three months by the Fiscal, who urged him to give up his religion. The drugged food was again administered and Ramé reduced to such a state of depression that he contemplated suicide. He was a strong-minded man and realized the state into which he was falling; so, as a desperate antidote, he made a harp by taking some of the boards from his bed and unpicking a pair of silk stockings. He unravelled more stockings and made a cap; and he found a way of making needles out of the boards of his bed.

After two years he was taken before the Tribunal again, and this time he found waiting for him, instead of the Inquisitor and Fiscal, a 'great many Ecclesiastics and lawyers'.

A Jesuit then told him before them all that God had chosen this opportunity to open his eyes, and had brought him to the Inquisition in order that his soul might be saved; he quoted the Parable of the Vineyard and how God had sent to seek for labourers in the morning, noon, and evening.

Ramé answered that he had read that Jesus Christ called the people to his preaching and never made use of secret prisons and fetters.

The ecclesiastics began to talk disparagingly of the Protestant religion and how it had been invented by Calvin who was a very 'ill man', to which Ramé retorted that he knew nothing of the religion of Calvin, for his own religion was that of Christ.

He was told that he was blind and rebellious to the will of God and was asked to choose, out of four men who were presented to him, an advocate who would defend him in his trial. He asked them how one of their men could defend him when he acted against their will and pleasure, and said that he would rely on his Saviour, Jesus Christ.

He was, however, forced to accept one, who immediately began to urge him to become a Catholic!

He was then returned to his cell. Each Saturday he was visited by an Inquisitor, Don Juan de Miel, and, he writes, when he was asked how he did, he generally answered that he did as well as any man could in such a place. And when the Inquisitor asked if he wanted anything, he replied: 'I want the patience of Job, the virtue of Joseph, the wisdom of Solomon, the resolution of Tobit, the repentance of David, justice from your tribunal and a quick expedition.'

He was kept in prison for another two years and was again made ill by the food which was given him, before he was taken before the Tribunal and sentenced to banishment from the kingdom of New-Spain; consequently he was put into the royal prison.

This royal prison was the old palace of Montezuma who had been Emperor of Mexico, and here Ramé's sentence was read to him, and he was asked to swear to tell nothing of what had happened to him at the hands of the Inquisition, and warned that if he did so he would be awarded two hundred lashes.

Ramé tells us that his reply was that, while he would undertake to say nothing whilst he was in the dominions of the King of Spain, when he returned to France it would be necessary to explain what had been happening to him. This they appeared to accept.

He was taken to another prison where he was fed well for a week, so that his health recovered and he regained his sight which he had almost lost; after that he was returned to the royal prison and, when he had been there a short while, he was sent to a village a few miles from Mexico City; and in this village he was set to work manufacturing cloth with criminals.

Among the workers was a man named Thomas. Ramé forgot his surname, but he knew that he came from Plymouth, so presumably he was a sailor who had fallen into the hands of the Inquisition. To save himself Thomas had become a Catholic, and as a penance was sent to work at the cloth factory. Thomas, having been taken into the Catholic Church, was sent to the Tribunal to give an account of the ceremony, and Ramé wrote a letter to the Tribunal which he persuaded Thomas to deliver. In it he reminded them that they had said he should be deported.

He had a reply that he must present a petition to the President of Criminal Affairs; this he did, and as a result he was taken back to prison and fettered; thus he remained for six more months.

He was then taken from prison and put on a mule which was to carry him to Vera Cruz. The animal was vicious and heavily loaded, and Ramé believed that the authorities intended that he should have a serious accident.

Arriving at Vera Cruz he was put into prison, but he met with a little good fortune there, for a man, for whom he had once worked in Vera Cruz, had heard of his sufferings and sent him food, gave him money to buy what he needed, and visited him twice a week.

Eventually he was taken to the quay and put aboard a ship for Havana which, after a stormy passage, he reached.

Here he was again put in prison, where he remained for another six months, being fed very badly, all the time being pestered to change his religion. When a captured Dutch ship, which had been renamed the *St Joseph* by the Spaniards, came into the harbour, he was put aboard, but as the ship could not sail immediately owing to the wind, Ramé was put into the stocks until she did.

After two months at sea they reached Cadiz, but Ramé was not allowed to go ashore and was still kept a close prisoner. He was later taken to Seville where he was once more imprisoned, and for six weeks he had scarcely anything to eat; only the English prisoners fared well for there were English merchants in the city who sent food for them.

When at length Ramé was sentenced to serve the King of Spain in Cadiz at whatever work the Governor of the city should find for him, he protested and demanded that his case should be set before the Tribunal of Madrid.

By this time many might have despaired of ever escaping but Ramé did not give up; he sent petitions to Madrid and managed to get a letter to his wife, and a French friend in Seville worked hard for him but without result. But eventually with the help of ambassadors and other Frenchmen in Spain, Ramé was released, turned out of prison without money and ordered to leave the country, but was given no means of doing so.

Fortunately for him, his French friends came to his aid, money was provided, and a ship was found, *The Loyalty of London*, which took him to England.

He arrived in England on 18th August, 1685.

He ends his account with the poignant words: 'God be praised; I was thought dead, but I am living.'

In his account Louis Ramé provides some interesting sidelights on incidents which he saw during his imprisonment. He tells of how in Holy Week people went to church in masks and whipped their own naked backs as they passed through the streets. These whippings were often so severe that the whipped backs were covered with blood. In procession they carried an image which represented Christ and another which represented the Virgin Mary. Masked men dressed in brilliant colours with tails affixed to their backs made gestures before the images. These men represented Jews who the people believed were born with tails because they had descended from those Jews who had crucified Christ.

He tells too that when he was in the prison of Vera Cruz, one hundred and eight buccaneers were captured, among whom were fourteen officers who were brought to the prison in which Ramé was kept. They were Protestants and therefore condemned to the stake.

When they were taken to the *quemadero* five of them suffered the fire, but the remaining nine declared their desire to become Catholics. They were brought back to the prison, allowed to wash, and all given clean shirts, feasted and told to choose godfathers. They were given plenty to drink, and were very merry because they believed they had come near to death and had saved their lives. Ramé tells us that he was invited to this dinner, and that his beard amused the newly-shaven men who called him 'Papas', a name, says Ramé, given to 'grave old learned men'. Ramé was allowed to shave his beard and everybody was very merry.

But, as soon as the feast was over, the new Catholics were hurried out to a place of execution where they were to be strangled.

Eight of the nine died, but the ninth, named John Morgan, was very fortunate. The rope about his neck broke, and when a new one was tried that broke also. There was a third attempt, which ended in failure; then were the executioners overcome with dread. John Morgan was pardoned, for all believed that he was a true convert and that it was the will of the Virgin Mary that he should not die.

Ramé also writes that on his journey from Vera Cruz to Mexico he saw near Mexico City a hot spring which flowed from the mountains. The legend was that the Virgin Mary appeared at this spot to an Indian who went to the Archbishop to explain that he had seen the Virgin and that she had told him of the spring; but the Archbishop did not believe his talk of visions.

Once again the Virgin Mary appeared to the Indian and insisted that he go to the Archbishop and tell him of the existence of the spring; the Indian replied that the Archbishop would not listen to him, whereupon the Virgin gathered some roses from where before that moment there had been no roses and put them inside the Indian's blanket which he wore as a cloak.

The Archbishop changed his mind when he saw the flowers, and a chapel was built on the spot where the encounter was supposed to have taken place.

Below the mountain was built a magnificent church in which were gold and silver lamps and pearls and emeralds which Ramé estimated must have been worth something in the region of a million pieces of eight. The name of the church was Our Lady of Guadalupa, and those who did not go there every Saturday were not considered to be good Christians and were in danger of being regarded with suspicion. Crutches lay about the entrance to the church. They had belonged, Ramé tells us, to people who were said to have come as cripples and had been cured by the Virgin.


There are three Inquisitors of the Mexican Tribunal who are remembered for their special cruelty. It is known that they even went so far as to request the Supreme Council in Spain for permission to relax ten prisoners who had asked for reconciliation to the Church.

There was a prisoner, Doña Catalina de Campos, who became very ill in prison and begged these Inquisitors to give her some comfort; she declared that she had always been a good Catholic and would continue so to be; the cell in which she was lodged was particularly noisome, being overrun with vermin.

The answer of the Inquisitors to this request was to send the woman back to her cell. A few days later she was found dead, her body gnawed by rats.

The names of these three were Juan Saenz de Mañozca, Francis de Estrada y Esvobedo and Bernabé de la Higuera y Amarilla. (Lea, *The Inquisition in the Spanish Dependencies*.)

Another very sad case is that of Gabriel de Granada, a boy, thirteen years old, whose trial (or process – the Inquisitorial description) took place from 1642 to 1645.

This boy was arrested on suspicion of being an 'Observer of the Law of Moses' and when he was prevailed upon to testify against over a hundred people, including all the members of his family, he told the Inquisitors how his mother had initiated him into the Law of Moses and had told him that it was the true religion. His mother eventually starved herself to death in her cell, presumably in order to avoid a more frightful death; other members of the family and their friends also suffered.

As for Gabriel himself, he was told that he would be pardoned for his crimes because he had shown contrition and repentance and had begged forgiveness from God. This he had done, of course, by betraying to indescribable misery those who had been good to him – but that was what was required of a 'good' Catholic by the Inquisition.

God, he was told, did not desire the death of the sinner but that he should be converted and live, and therefore was to be admitted to reconciliation.

He was to go forth to the *auto* with other penitents 'without waist-band and bonnet and with a penitential habit of yellow cloth with two red bars in the form of St Andrew's Cross, and carrying a green wax candle in his hands, where this our sentence shall be read to him, and publicly abjure his said errors which before us he hath confessed and all species whatsoever of heresy and apostasy'.

Gabriel was condemned to wear over his clothes the *sanbenito* for a year while he was kept a prisoner, and every Sunday and feast day he was to go to hear high Mass, and on Saturdays he was to go in pilgrimage to the church where he was to recite the paternoster five times and the Ave Maria, Creed and *Salve Regina*. He was to confess and receive the Sacrament at Christmas, Epiphany and Easter every year of his life and was to be banished from the West Indies and from Seville, Madrid and the King's Court.

He was to leave Vera Cruz as soon as possible and present himself at the Tribunal of the Holy Office in Seville, where he would be told where to go to work out the rest of his sentence. He was never to hold any public or honourable office either ecclesiastical or secular; he was to wear neither gold, silver, pearls, nor precious stones, nor silk camelot nor fine cloth; nor was he to travel on horseback nor carry arms.

This was the sentence on the boy who had betrayed his family and friends. (*Trial of Gabriel de Granada*. Translated from the original by David Fergusson in the Publications of the American Jewish Historical Society.)

Sebastian Domingo was a Negro slave and sixty years of age when he fell into the hands of the Inquisition. His wife had been sold separately and his owner, fearing that he might attempt to escape in order to join his wife, insisted on his marrying another woman.

The Inquisition stepped in and he was arrested for bigamy and incarcerated in the Inquisition of La Puebla de los Angeles.

So many people had been taken into this prison that, no doubt because Sebastian's offence was not one of heresy and probably because he was the sort of man who would make a good servant, he was put to work in the prison.

All servants of the Inquisition were sworn to secrecy and not allowed to have communication with the prisoners. It might have been that Sebastian was an ignorant man and did not understand these rules; however he spoke to a male prisoner through his grating and agreed to take a note to this man's wife. When the wife received the letter she was so delighted and grateful to Sebastian that she rather naturally offered him some money – which he accepted.

There were of course spies everywhere in the prison and the prisoner's wife was herself soon a prisoner – her offence being that she had received a letter from her husband. As for Sebastian, he was accused of two crimes: first taking a letter from a prisoner to his wife, and then receiving a reward for doing so.

Poor Sebastian was sentenced to two hundred lashes and six years in the galleys in Spain, but if he could not go to Spain (and the Inquisitors knew some reason why he could not) he was to be sold for a hundred dollars, which should go into the exchequer of the Holy Office.

The sale must, of course, be only for a certain time, for Sebastian belonged to the master whom he had been serving at the time of his arrest. The Inquisition decided they would sell him for ten years and in case he should die under the lashes, and thus the money be lost to the Inquisition, he was to be forgiven the lashes.

This was done, for the Inquisitors did not consider that by selling a slave who belonged to someone else they were committing a fraud. But no doubt they assured themselves that as it was done in the name of the Inquisition, that exonerated them from blame.

It is very interesting to compare these harsh punishments with those inflicted on priests.

The prevailing sin among priests was that of solicitation, and the punishment for this naturally fell within the scope of the Inquisition.

This seduction of women who came to confess their sins was known as *solicitatio ad turpia* and had given great trouble to the Church ever since there had been confession. Many priests – condemned to celibacy – found temptation irresistible when they had young women kneeling at their feet, confessing their sins, real or concocted. In the middle of the sixteenth century the box with the grille was invented, but there were many cases of solicitation after that.

In 1558 Archbishop Guerrero of Granada called the Pope's attention to this recurring sin and asked that measures be taken to suppress it. Solicitation came under the jurisdiction of the Inquisition when it was agreed that anyone who committed this sin could not be perfect in his faith.

Priests were usually treated with great leniency by their fellow priests, and in 1626 Urban VIII was asking all Archbishops to warn priests of their responsibilities. Little attention was paid to his words, and when these philandering confessors were discovered they were given the lightest possible sentences.

It was suggested that there should be two witnesses against a priest before he could be accused, and as the offence would by its very nature be rarely committed in the presence of a third party this was making denial easy for the priest. But even this was considered harsh, and it was suggested that a priest should be found guilty of four offences before he was sentenced.

Paul IV instructed the Inquisition in the Spanish Dominions to deal with priests who were accused of solicitation; but even when a priest was found guilty he did not appear in the public *autos de fé,* unless of course he was to lose his orders. He was conducted to a room and there, behind closed doors and in the presence of a few priests, his sentence was declared to him.

There was, as can well be imagined, less restraint among the priests in such lands as Mexico than among those in Spain. It was generally believed by numbers of the settlers that while there might be some sin in seducing a Spanish girl this was not the case with the Indians. (The natives of Mexico did not come under the jurisdiction of the Inquisition, for the settlers believed that they were not intelligent enough to understand religion, and so were left to the care of the Bishops who were almost certain to be more gentle than the Holy Office.)

Consider the case of Fray Juan de Saldaña which was brought to light in 1583. Saldaña had attempted to seduce an Indian girl, and when she refused him he had had her arrested and flogged, threatening to repeat the floggings until she accepted his attentions. The girl finally agreed.

Saldaña held a high position in his Franciscan Order and, although only thirty-three years of age, was guardian of the Convent of Suchipila. The convent soon became a happy hunting-ground for this amorous Franciscan, and during confession he seduced three sisters in turn.

He made no secret of his behaviour – rather did he boast of his prowess. He said that he had not only seduced Spanish girls but Indians, and not only in the convent but wherever he heard confessions.

His friends thought it advisable to warn him, and reminded him that such conduct could bring him before the Tribunal of the Inquisition. He merely laughed at the warnings, and retorted that the only punishment which would be meted out for such offences as he had committed would be a dozen strokes of the discipline and a year's suspension from his guardianship of the convent – which of course was a small price to pay for the fun he was having.

The Inquisition could not remain blind to the vices of such a blatant sinner, and he was eventually brought before the Tribunal. Blithely he confessed his sins, and it almost seems that he was as ready to boast of his exploits to the Inquisitors as he had to others. Yes, he had seduced several Spanish women during confession, as well as seven Indians. He admitted that previously he had been prevented from confessing Spanish women because of similar offences but, as guardian of the convent, he had naturally been the confessor.

His sentence was that he should be whipped 'during the space of a *miserere*', deprived of the opportunity of hearing confessions, suspended from his order for six years, retired to a convent for two and then banished from Guadalajara for six years. (David Fergusson.)

Presumably when that time had elapsed he might continue with his activities. It is astonishing to recall that hideous tortures and burning alive were inflicted on people for not eating pork, for staining their nails with henna, or for praying to Christ instead of the Virgin Mary.

The case of Fray Juan de Saldaña is by no means an isolated one. There were numerous cases of solicitation, and not only in Mexico but in other dependencies and Spain itself. And in all such the penalties were astonishingly light when compared with those inflicted for other crimes.

In 1619 the Mexican Inquisitors stated in a letter to the Supreme Council that solicitation occurred very frequently in their part of the world and that it was regarded by many as trivial.

Lea suggested that the punishment for solicitation became less severe as time passed, and cites the case of Fray Francisco Diego de Zarate as an instance of this.

Fray Francisco was a Franciscan and President of the Mission of Santa Maria de los Angeles of Rio Blanca, and therefore a man of some standing.

He was brought before the Tribunal on charges of solicitation in the year 1721, when a hundred and twenty-six cases of solicitation were proved against him in respect of fifty-six women. It was said that he never failed to attempt the seduction of any woman who came to him to confess.

He might have gone on indefinitely, but he eventually tried to seduce a woman who was determined to resist him. He was equally determined not to be resisted. He declared that if she did not become his mistress he would have her and her family banished from Rio Blanca.

The woman went away and told all her friends what the priest had tried and failed to do and how he proposed to punish her and her family because she had resisted him. There was such a scandal that it was impossible for the Inquisition to ignore, and thus Fray Francisco was arrested and brought before the Tribunal of the Holy Office.

He was then accused of seducing numerous women. He appears to have been a little hurt because according to his reckoning he had seduced far more than appeared on the Inquisitors' list. He therefore corrected this, having been in a better position to keep the score.

The sentence was that he should receive a circular discipline, that he should never hear confession again, and should be deprived of his high office in his Order. He was to refrain from celebrating Mass for six months and spend two years in seclusion in a convent; and the first year he was to spend in a cell, living on bread and water (only on Fridays and Saturdays though) and he should have the last place in the choir and at the refectory.

It may be that even these sentences were not carried out, for in 1666 a letter was written to the Supreme Council in which it was stated that certain sentences on frailes had been rescinded.

William Harris Rule, in his *History of the Inquisition, Volume II,* states that information he has acquired makes it possible for him to remind us of another punishment which was used by the Inquisition in Mexico. This is known as 'Walling up' and consists of building four walls about a living person, giving that person just enough room to stand or sit, and leaving them thus to die.

He tells us that when the Inquisition came to an end, part of an old palace, which had been the headquarters, fell into the hands of the Rev. Dr William Butler, a Missionary of the Methodist Episcopal Church. Realizing that he was in possession of part of what had once housed the Inquisitor-General of Mexico, Dr Butler was very eager to examine his property in the hope of discovering relics of the Inquisition.

In the basement was a long gallery and, when he had the paving stones removed, he found about two hundred skeletons. They lay side by side, 'shoulder to foot and foot to shoulder alternately'.

The bones were removed and the stones relaid. There is no suggestion from the Rev. Dr Butler nor from William Harris Rule, D.D., that these were not the skeletons of people who had died natural deaths, but it does seem strange that they should have been buried in this manner.

Another discovery was made.

The inside of the main wall was for a large part unbroken by any windows or doors, and on examination it was seen that in places the bricks had been broken away and small spaces were revealed – chambers (or cupboards) in which a person of average size could barely stand upright. Dr Butler, intrigued by this discovery, had the rest of the wall tapped, and in four places it was found to be hollow. The bricks were removed and the skeletons of four bodies were discovered – three men and a woman. The woman was lying down, and at her feet was that which was presumed to have been a child.

These remains were taken to the museum in the city of Mexico, 'where,' said William Harris Rule, writing in 1874, 'they may still now be seen.'

He goes on to say that these niches must have been left in the wall when it was built – for the purpose of walling up. None of the four walls about these small closets let in light or air, and there was naturally no possibility of passing food to those incarcerated therein.

The four bodies which were found were dressed alike, and it is to be presumed that this was the regulation dress for those who were to die this way. It may have been, suggests Rule, that the treatment of men and women was slightly different and that the longer and lower cavities were provided for women, who

87

were allowed the privilege of dying in a recumbent position.

The heads of all four had been shaved, the arms bent at the elbows and bound; and there were fetters about the ankles.

One of the bodies was seated on a stone in his niche. This may have been due to the fact that he had been so violently tortured that it was impossible for him to stand.

When these bodies were discovered, the flesh was not entirely decayed, and this leads Rule to the conjecture that they had been walled up only a few years before the discovery. He submits that this ghastly form of death-dealing may have been adopted because the power of the Inquisition was fast waning in the nineteenth century and the people, becoming more enlightened and consequently more humane, would no longer tolerate the sight of human beings burning at the stake. Therefore this horrible method of murder was conceived and used by the men of the Holy Office because it could be carried out secretly within the precincts of the Holy House itself.

It must be said however that it is not absolutely certain that these walled-up people were the victims of the Inquisition. Yet they were discovered in the old palace which was the headquarters of the Inquisition, and the fact that they must have been put there in that century is very strong circumstantial evidence in favour of the belief that this hideous form of murder was used by the Inquisition in Mexico.

## CHAPTER SIX

## PERU

The Inquisition was established in Peru in 1570, when Servan de Cerezuela came to Lima to set up the tribunal. Before this date the power to judge heresy was in the hands of the Bishops and, as had been the case in other countries since the earliest days, there was antagonism between the Bishops and officials of the Inquisition; and in 1584 the Inquisitor of Peru, Ulloa, complained bitterly to the Supreme Council in Spain of the secret action of the Bishops in writing disparagingly of him to the King. The Bishops had every good reason to do this; but even if they had not, it seems certain that the antagonism towards the Inquisition was natural, for with its coming it usurped much of their power.

Ulloa was preceded by Servan de Cerezuela, who was selected by Inquisitor-General Espinosa in 1569 to go to Peru, in the same manner as Doctor Moya de Contreras had been selected for Mexico. He was instructed to make ready to leave at once, and with him were to sail the Viceroy, Francisco de Toledo, and another Inquisitor, Dr Andrés de Bustamente.

They sailed in March 1569 but by June, when they had reached Nombre de Dios, their money had run out, and it was necessary to raise more. Meanwhile Andrés de Bustamente died.

During the delay Cerezuela tried a few cases, and when he reached Panama the Viceroy and the judges were commanded to take the oath of allegiance to the Inquisition.

Cerezuela arrived at Lima on the 28th of November.

The usual pattern was followed: the ceremonies to inspire and terrify the people, the recital of the Edict of Faith which was followed by numerous denunciations and arrests; and by 15th November, 1573, the first *auto de fé* was held.

Cerezuela was not a popular Inquisitor; there were continual complaints of his inexperience, and it was very quickly felt that he should be replaced. Consequently Antonio Gutiérrez de Ulloa arrived to take over in March 1571, and it could not have been long before it was realized that the incompetence of Cerezuela was preferable to the villainies of Ulloa.

The latter was soon engaged in amours, and even went so far as to keep a permanent mistress whom he allowed to influence him in his judgments.

He wandered the streets at night (not in his Inquisitorial robes but dressed as a gay gallant) in search of adventures, was engaged in many a brawl and enjoyed the company of prostitutes. When he was caught, *in flagrante delicto,* by a husband, he assumed the role of Inquisitor, informing the husband of what could happen to him if he fell into the hands of the Inquisition – which he would certainly do if he sought to criticize the conduct of Inquisitor Ulloa.

Another husband, in similar circumstances, was bolder; he murdered his wife and threatened Ulloa, in spite of the fact that he was Inquisitor. This was the cause of great scandal.

Money interested him as much as women; he had an interest in the quicksilver mines in Guancavelica, and a great deal of money which should have gone to the Treasury of Spain found its way into his pocket.

So many complaints about this man reached the Supreme Council that it was decided to send a *visitador* to Lima to discover the truth. This man, Juan Ruiz de Prado, was given all the authority he needed to prosecute any member of the Inquisition in Peru.

The Viceroy, Villar, who had been largely instrumental in calling in the services of Prado, expected him to be his ally, but when he arrived Prado seemed more inclined to form a friendship with Ulloa, the very man whose actions he had come to investigate.

At the time of Prado's coming Sir Francis Drake's cousin, John Drake, and Richard Farrel were wrecked in the River Plate, and as they were heretics they were brought before the Inquisition. The capture of two such men seemed, in the Viceroy's opinion, to offer an unusually good opportunity for discovering the whereabouts of English shipping, and he wanted them brought to him for questioning. Ulloa, however, insisted that they were the prisoners of the Inquisition and that he could not release Drake and Farrel without express orders from the Suprema in Spain. As this would take about a year to obtain, Villar pointed out the folly of the decision, for he needed the information immediately.

Then came the alarm (unfounded) that the English ships were sighted, and Villar called up all men available to defend Callao against the English. Both Ulloa and Prado, making sure that the offices of the Inquisition were protected, gave orders that the men were not to obey Villar.

Exasperated, Villar pointed out that the men would be defending the Inquisition as well as the city.

But Ulloa and Prado had their way; together they rendered the Viceroy powerless and took charge of the city. Villar realized the uselessness of attempting to govern when the Inquisition was more powerful than the state.

Prado at this time was determined to stand by Ulloa, and when a man from whom Ulloa had borrowed a great deal of money asked for its return and, not getting it, produced a writ against the Inquisitor, it was Prado who had the poor man arrested, suspended from his benefice (he was a priest), and sentenced to four years' confinement, during which he was so maltreated that he died.

The friendship between Prado and Ulloa suddenly ceased; and from that time the end of Ulloa's pleasant way of life was in sight. Prado seemed suddenly to remember the reason he had been sent to Peru and set about examining all the evidence which had been accumulating against the man who had until now been his friend; and as a result he drew up 216 charges against Ulloa.

He discovered the scandals concerning many women, and how Ulloa had taken control of the quicksilver mines by reminding all other bidders that he was at the head of the Inquisition and that they could guess what would happen to them if they bid against him; as a result he and his brother and a friend had been granted concessions at a much lower price than the other bidders had offered.

Ulloa then began to enquire into the peccadilloes of Prado,

that he might expose them. He accused him of shady financial dealings.

The Suprema in Spain sent orders to both men. Prado was to leave Peru at once and return to Spain; 118 of the 216 charges against Ulloa were accepted, and he was to be suspended from his office for five years, pay a fine, and return to Spain for a reprimand by the Inquisitor-General.

Prado had proposed some reforms and, when the Supreme Council studied these, it was decided that it might be a good thing to try some of them. Prado was therefore instructed not to leave Peru, but by the time the order came he had already sailed for Spain in accordance with the original instructions.

Ulloa in the meantime was in no hurry to obey the summons to return to Spain. The Licentiate, Antonio Ordóñez y Flores, arrived on 4th February, 1594, to take Ulloa's place, and then Ulloa began his very slow journey across the country. He still behaved as though he were Inquisitor, and terrified the people in the villages through which he passed.

An example of his behaviour is given by Diego Vanegas who was the son of the judge of the Contratacion of Seville.

Ulloa had stopped at Cuzco and was lodging with Francisco de Loaysa. One of the latter's servants boasted in the presence of Vanegas and his friends, who were talking together in the public square, that staying in his master's house was the Inquisitor, Ulloa, whose power exceeded that of anybody in Peru. He then began to tell a story which illustrated the power of Ulloa, and Vanegas lightly remarked that he and his friends were not really interested and did not wish to hear any more.

Vanegas was arrested and taken before Ulloa, who called some twenty of his men and told them to kill this man who had spoken disparagingly of the Inquisition and its Inquisitors. The men would have obeyed and Vanegas would have lost his life if Doña Mariana de Loaysa had not begged them to refrain from killing a man in her house. Ulloa, susceptible to the pleas of some women, agreed to spare the life of Vanegas and ordered that he should be given five hundred lashes. On further protests from Doña Mariana, Ulloa agreed that there should be only two hundred, but on the lady's further protests against violence he said that Vanegas should be banished.

When Ulloa left Cuzco word reached him that Vanegas, who was in bed recovering from the beating which had been given him, had declared his intention of going to Spain that he might report in person the ill conduct of Ulloa. Furious, Ulloa sent some of his men back to Cuzco to arrest Vanegas, who was dragged from his bed and taken to prison, where he remained for four months. After that he was sentenced to serve for three years as a soldier on the frontier or in the galleys.

Vanegas managed to escape, and went to Lima where he saw the Viceroy, explained what had happened and was given permission to go to Spain to make a complaint against Ulloa. (Lea.)

Ulloa meanwhile had no intention of going to Spain to be reprimanded, so he complained of ill health and his inability to travel. Perhaps there was some truth in this, for he died in Lima in 1597, nearly three years after the Suprema had accepted the charges against him.

Peru was unfortunate in her Inquisitors, and although Ulloa may have been one of the most villainous, those who followed him were not noted for their virtues. When it is realized that these men were kings in their territory, that they had the power to excommunicate, that they could stand in judgment and only the Suprema, far away in Spain, could call them to account for their actions, it is perhaps understandable.

The Inquisition had been set up in the Spanish colonies to protect them from Protestant infiltration, but there was little for it to do in this respect, although some of the victims who appeared at the *autos de fé* were sailors who had been shipwrecked or taken prisoner at sea.

In 1581 and 1587 two Flemings, Jan Bernal and Miguel del Pilar were arrested, accused of being Protestants and were both burned alive; and in the first *auto de fé* (1573) two Protestants appeared, Joan Bautista and Mateo Salado. But these were few, and after 1587 another does not appear until 1625.

The Inquisition found itself more concerned with Jews, for many of this race had come to the colonies in the hope of making their fortunes as well as finding a haven where they would be safe from the persecution of the old country. So many opportunities did the Jews see in these new and as yet unexploited lands, that they overcame all the difficulties which were put in their way and many emigrated. Thus they provided the Inquisition with the victims it sought.

In 1626 one of the most interesting of the cases against a Jew began, although it did not end until 1639, a typical example of the circumlocution at Inquisitorial trials. This concerned a Francisco Maldonado de Silva, who was a greatly respected surgeon in Concepcion de Chile, and of Portuguese origin.

Francisco had been brought up as a Catholic, for his father had been a prisoner of the Inquisition which had allowed him to become reconciled to the Church and ordered him to bring up his children – Francisco, Isabel and another girl – as Christians.

When Francisco was eighteen he read the *Scrutinium Scripturarum*, a book which had been written by one of the greatest Jewish teachers, Rabbi Selemoh Ha-Levi, who was converted to Catholicism in 1390 and became Pablo de Santa Maria. He was later regent of Spain and Bishop of Cartagena and Burgos. This book was supposed to be written to help Jews to become Catholics but it had the reverse effect upon Francisco.

He spoke to his father about these doubts, and his father's advice was that he should study the Bible, and at the same time he gave him some instruction in the Law of Moses.

It was not long before Francisco decided that he would accept the Jewish Faith and no other, although he kept this a secret, and his mother, two sisters, and even his wife had no idea that he had reverted to the faith of his fathers.

The family appear to have been an affectionate one and Francisco was particularly fond of his sister Isabel (who was about two years younger than he was). This must have been the case because it was to Isabel that he eventually confided the news of his conversion. She was at this time thirty-three years of age, and, it seems, a devout Catholic, for when she heard her brother's confession she was thrown into an agony of uncertainty.

Again and again she had been taught the duty of a good Catholic: there was no loyalty to be set against that due to the Church.

First she told her confessor, and this gave rise to further misery, for her confessor informed her that the only way she could expiate the sin of listening to her brother, was by denouncing him to the Inquisition.

Isabel wrestled with her love for her brother and her fear of eternal damnation, and eventually fear was the conqueror. As a result Francisco was arrested and brought before the Tribunal. He was firm in his resolve to cling to the Law of Moses, and efforts to make him return to the Catholic Church failed.

His wretchedness must have equalled that of his sister, for he knew that no one was aware that he had changed his religion, except Isabel, and that she was the one who had betrayed him.

Boldly he admitted to the Tribunal that he was a Jew and that he intended to die in that faith; with the result that he was branded a relaxed heretic and sentenced to death at the stake.

Life in prison had weakened him and he was very ill. He asked that instead of his ration of bread he should be given maize husks. This was done, and he made a rope which enabled him to escape from his room and visit other Jewish prisoners.

During the years he spent in prison he made two books out of scraps of paper, pens from egg-shells and ink from charcoal.

It was thirteen years before he was finally brought out of prison and burned alive. The books he had made were hung about his neck and burned with him. (Lea and *Publications of the American Jewish Historical Society*.)

The *auto de fé* at which Francisco Maldonado de Silva was burned was the most important that had yet been held in Peru, because on this occasion suffered many Jews who had been rounded up in what was called the '*complicidad grande*'.

At this time there were many Jews in Peru, and their presence was being felt, for they were beginning to control the commerce of the country. Envy brought them to the notice of the Inquisition, and in 1636 almost a hundred had been arrested, and had there been bigger prisons available there would have been more arrests.

These prisoners were almost all wealthy men and in some cases they brought great temptation to their jailers. There is a recorded case of one, Bartolomé de Pradeda, on whom suspicion fell because he suddenly began acquiring a great deal of property. The matter was investigated, and the discovery was made that Bartolomé's wealth had been acquired in exchange for certain favours.

The Inquisition was never really very severe with its own; bribery, solicitation – such sins were venial in their eyes compared with heresy. So Bartolomé was merely dismissed; but the temptation proved too great for his successor and he too soon followed Bartolomé into retirement, as did *his* successor and two others who came after him. The Inquisitors by that time had realized the need for a little more severity, and two of the three last, who did not hold very high positions in the Inquisition, were punished – one sent to the galleys, the other to do penance in an *auto*.

The treatment of prisoners concerned in the *complicidad grande* was very severe. A twenty-seven-year-old woman, Murcia de Luna, died under torture; her sister Isabel de Luna, aged eighteen, was stripped to the waist and given a hundred lashes in the streets with her mother who was treated in the same manner. A boy of eighteen Enrique Jorge Tavares, refused to confess, though cruelly tortured, and was so ill-used that he became insane.

One very rich man, Manuel Bautista Pérez, who was the foremost merchant in Lima, was burned alive. He had made himself a leader of a group, and meetings had been held in his house. The owner of silver mines and plantations, he was a great prize, and his carriage alone brought in the sum of 3,400 pesos. His attempt to commit suicide was unsuccessful and he went bravely to his death.

Another victim of this purge was Antonio Cordero who was a merchant's clerk. Another merchant denounced him to the Inquisition, so this may have been a case of business rivalry. The merchant, de Salazar, reported to the Inquisition that he had gone into the shop of which Cordero was in charge and had been told by Cordero that customers were not served on Saturdays. He also declared that he had on a certain Friday seen Cordero at a meal in the shop and asked him why he did not eat bacon; to which Nordero was alleged to have replied that his father and grandfather had never eaten bacon, so neither would he.

The Inquisition decided to arrest him on suspicion and sent one of their familiars into the shop as though he were a customer. The familiar then forced Cordero into a room behind the shop and locked him in; after dark Cordero was conducted to the secret prison of the Inquisition.

It was not generally known that he had been made a prisoner, so secretly was the arrest made, and it was believed that Cordero, knowing the Inquisition was on his trail, had fled from the city.

Cordero was tortured and implicated others, so that because a man refused to eat bacon and serve a customer on a Saturday, the lives of many people were either lost or ruined.

Another source of supply was the great body of mystics; and, as the people of Peru were as ready to accept miraculous wonders as the people of Spain, there appeared many *beatas* and holy men, and some of these encountered the suspicions of the Inquisition.

One of the most notorious of these *beatas* flourished in the 1560s. Her name was María Pizarro, and she declared that she had had a visitation from the Angel Gabriel, and that the Immaculate Conception had been revealed to her.

Among her admirers were two Jesuits who had been sent to Peru as missionaries; one of these men was Gerónimo Ruiz Portillo and the other Padre Luis López; the highly-respected Professor of Theology, Fray Francisco de la Cruz, was also among her admirers.

María was evidently a hysterical subject and believed that she was in contact with the Devil. The trouble started when one of her admirers, a Dominican, Fray Alonso Gasco, confessed that he had in his possession certain objects which had been blessed by the Devil.

As a result María was arrested and, when she was in prison and no doubt thought her end was near, she made her confession. She said that in the first place the Jesuit Padre Luis López had seduced her and that afterwards she was invited by the Devil to become his succubus, which she did.

Later she changed her confession and said that she had lied concerning López. She died before she could be brought to trial.

The denunciation of María Pizarro meant that many of her supporters were brought under suspicion, and among these was the Professor of Theology, Francisco de la Cruz. Under examination he persisted that he had believed María's revelations had come from the Angel Gabriel and that the doctrines which María had preached were true ones.

Many of these women who sought to set themselves apart from their fellows by their intimacy with the Trinity, the Virgin Mary, the angels and saints, followed this way of life because they enjoyed the limelight. Moreover it was an easy and very interesting method of earning a livelihood, for the woman – or man – who was endowed with such special powers was treated with the utmost respect by almost all, and rich gifts and presents frequently came their way. Some of them dedicated themselves to a life of privation, but others wished to live full and sensuous lives; they wished to indulge in amorous relations with the opposite sex; and because of this they were obliged to formulate a new doctrine, which was that there was no sin in making love and therefore priests and holy women could indulge in it as freely as they wished.

De la Cruz, who upheld these beliefs – and even went so far as to teach them – was clearly in the eyes of the Inquisition guilty of heresy.

By a married woman he had had a son who strutted about the city boasting that he was the Son of God. This child was captured by the Inquisitors and shipped to Panama where he was put into stern hands to be brought up in a fitting manner.

Meanwhile de la Cruz was taken to prison, tortured and finally condemned to the stake. It is believed that he asked for reconciliation at the last moment and was strangled.

Padre Luis López was a bold man. He dared to say that de la Cruz had been ill-treated by the Inquisition, since he was clearly insane. For this he was arrested. The case against him was that he had seduced María Pizarro in the first place, that he was guilty of solicitation on many occasions, and that he had actually written a pamphlet to the effect that Philip II had no right to take possession of Peru.

The last charge was treason and outside the scope of the

Inquisition which had only to deal with the criticism of itself, the seduction of María, and the solicitation.

López confessed that he had seduced women in the confessional, and he was given a scourging during the space of two *misereres*, imprisoned, and then sent to Spain. I can find no record of what happened to him there.

So the persecution continued to the detriment of Peru's prosperity. In 1813 the Inquisition was suppressed, but in 1814 it was established once more, only to be finally suppressed in 1820.

The number of cases dealt with by the Inquisition in Peru seems astonishingly small. Henry Charles Lea quotes Teodoro Marino as stating that 3,000 were tried in the 250 years of its existence. His researches though (Lea points out), which were exhaustive, enabled him to name only 1,474 cases.

If Lea is right and there were even fewer cases than Marino believed, the folly of establishing the Inquisition is even more obvious. It flourished at enormous expense; it had an adverse effect on the trade of the country; but even if these figures are accepted, for every one man who was brought before the Tribunal thousands feared to be taken there. So that if physical torture was carried out on comparatively few people the whole nation could never have felt entirely at ease. For how could they be sure when, in the darkness of the night, there would not come that ominous knocking on the door?

## CHAPTER SEVEN

# NAPLES

When Ferdinand conquered Naples the Papal Inquisition had previously been set up there by Charles of Anjou, and after the Aragonese robbed the House of Anjou of its possession, the Inquisition was allowed to remain as long as its members understood that it was second in importance to the crown. For this reason it languished.

When Ferdinand appeared on the scene, Pope Julius II was endeavouring to establish an Inquisition which should be under the wing of the Papacy. This was naturally not to Ferdinand's taste and he planned to introduce the Spanish Inquisition into Naples.

All preparations for doing this were made, but Ferdinand's object was not achieved. There is no detailed information as to why this should have been so; but it was probably due to the fact that there was great opposition in Naples; and because the inhabitants were known for their fiery dispositions, Ferdinand was too wise to force the Inquisition on them as soon as he had acquired dominion over them.

Ferdinand contented himself by persecuting the Jews in Naples. The Neapolitans, however, did not hate the Jews as the Spaniards had, and the persecutions began in a leisurely manner; the order of expulsion was not entirely carried out until 1540, when the Emperor Charles was in command. Large numbers of these Jews found their way to Turkey; but the exodus, like those which took place from Spain, resulted in great misfortune for thousands. There were the usual slaughterings and misery; and many were captured and sold into slavery. François Premier showed kindness to them, for when many of them appeared in Marseilles he allowed them to settle in the Levant without making any charge for this – which was a very generous act, since the French exchequer, like most, was in need of constant replenishment. This expulsion was followed by the usual disadvantages, and in Naples prosperity was undermined.

In the early fourteenth century the Waldenses had settled in the mountains of Calabria and Apulia; they cultivated the land, made it prosperous and lived peaceably for more than 200 years. When the Inquisition grew to power its eye was turned on these people, and Charles V was told that he should not allow them to continue in Heresy. Charles was less interested in making trouble among an industrious section of the community on the grounds of religion than his son was to be, and little was done about these people.

But by 1560 the Waldenses were once more attracting attention and Rome sent an Inquisitor, Valerio Malvicino da Piazenza, to San Sisto, La Guardia and Montalto to study the beliefs of the people. Valerio ordered them to accept the Catholic Faith, which they refused to do. San Sisto was first dealt with, for the population had taken up arms. San Sisto itself was burned, the men were slaughtered, and the women and children submitted to brutal outrage.

Many of the inhabitants of La Guardia and Montalto, who had also revolted, were sent before a tribunal. They were tortured, and there followed an *auto de fé* on 11th June, 1561.

A letter exists which was written on the day of this *auto de fé* by an observer who was a Catholic (Lea, *The Inquisition in the Spanish Dependencies*). The victims were led one by one into the open, their eyes covered by a blood-spattered bandage which had been used by the previous victim. In the public square their throats were cut, their bodies quartered and the fragments affixed to poles which had been set up from one end of Calabria to the other. This observer writes as though the sight shocked him deeply, but another faithful Catholic who witnessed the scene wrote that the sight was one to inspire the heretic with fear while it confirmed the believer in in his faith. It is easy to understand the former statement, but why the brutality of a sect should make its doctrines more convincing it is difficult to see. Eighty-eight people were treated in this way and seven, who had not broken down under violent torture and had refused to relinquish their beliefs, were burned alive. A hundred elderly women were condemned to death; and the total number of casualties on this occasion was calculated to be 1,600. How the rest died we cannot be sure, but it seems likely that they suffered in the same brutal way.

A reward of ten crowns per person was offered for the return of those who sought to escape, and this brought in men and women in their hundreds. From Rome came instructions that the *auto* of 1561 had been conducted in too brutal a fashion and liberation was advised. It appears that this advice was not accepted; more prisoners were sent to the galleys and the five leaders of the revolt were burned alive after their bodies had been covered with pitch that their sufferings might be increased. All children under fifteen were taken from their parents and put with Catholic families.

The Inquisition was more stern with La Guardia than it had been with San Sisto, because San Sisto had been guilty of a revolt against authority, whereas La Guardia was entirely heretic. Many of the inhabitants went to the stake, many were sentenced to the galleys, and the entire community were condemned to wear the *sanbenito* and to hear Mass thus garbed every day. No more than six people were allowed to meet together and their native speech was to be replaced by Italian.

The Waldenses who lived in the Apulia district were treated less harshly. The more obstinate went to the stake and some to the galleys, but the majority of the population became reconciled and the conditions imposed upon them were apparently acceptable. It may have been that both sides had realized the folly of what had happened in Calabria, where the land had been laid waste and there had been so much death and destruction.

This was the work of the Papal Inquisition; and although in the case of the Waldenses it had acted in as barbarous a manner as the Spanish Inquisition, it grew milder as the years passed, until its suppression in the eighteenth century.

## CHAPTER EIGHT

# SICILY

The Spanish Inquisition was established in Sicily in 1487. Sicily, of course, in the fifteenth century, belonged to Aragon; and until Torquemada, then Inquisitor-General of Aragon, sent his Inquisitor to the island it had been under the supervision of the Papal Inquisition. This had become too lax for the zealous Torquemada to tolerate and, on 18th August, 1487, the island celebrated the introduction of the Spanish Inquisition by an *auto de fé*.

Torquemada's Inquisition was mainly concerned with the destruction of the Jews, and this unfortunate race was driven from Sicily at the time of the great exodus of 1492.

The people of Sicily found the Spanish Inquisition more zealous and more severe than the Papal Inquisition, and they grew restive. By 1516 – at the time of Ferdinand's death – they were ready to rise against the Viceroy, Hugo de Moncada and the Inquisitor, Melchor Cervera, who had arrived two years before with strict instructions from Torquemada to obey in every detail the rules which he had laid down.

The barbarous rule of the Viceroy had reduced the islanders to great poverty, for he had cornered the wheat production and exported it, thus bringing starvation to Sicily. He was afraid, when he heard of Ferdinand's death, that he would be removed from his office, for he knew that the people would clamour for his dismissal; so he sought to withhold the news from the Sicilians, but it leaked out and the mob attacked his palace. The Viceroy, in the disguise of a lackey, managed to escape, and sailed across to Messina.

Having lost the Viceroy the people turned to the Inquisitor, Melchor Cervera, whom they had grown to hate. Cervera was not so fortunate as the Viceroy, Hugo de Moncada, had been, and would have been torn to pieces if he had not, to protect himself, grasped and held aloft a consecrated Host in a monstrance; and although he was jeered at by the people, they were superstitious enough to regard him as immune from their attack while he held such an object. Thus he too was able to find a ship and escape.

The mob then turned its attention to the prison of the Inquisition, stormed the building, freed the prisoners and scattered the records.

After that three years elapsed during which the Inquisition ceased to exist in Sicily.

The case of Cervera was examined, but as usual the Inquisition was lenient with its servants, and in 1519 he was sent back to the island.

During the following five or six years *autos de fé* were celebrated at the rate of approximately one a year, but the numbers executed were not large, perhaps on account of the small population.

The numbers of those who suffered death at the stake are given as: in 1519, 5; 1520, 5; 1521, 1; 1524, 5; 1525, 5; 1526, 5.

Inquisitors outside Spain appear to be more often accused of bribery and corruption than those living close to the alert eyes of the Suprema. Inquisitors took bribes called 'presents' from so many people that it was noticed that while many were sentenced to the galleys they did not all go there; and others who were condemned to wear the *sanbenito* escaped doing so. It was not very difficult to divert funds, which should have gone to the Inquisition, into the pockets of individual Inquisitors; and there were continual complaints.

The Inquisition continued active however after the Treaty of Utrecht (1713) when Sicily passed to Savoy; but even then the Inquisition which ruled Sicily continued to be the Spanish Inquisition.

Five years later Savoy exchanged Sicily for Sardinia, and the island fell into the hands of Austria. The Emperor of Austria was not content to allow the Inquisition to be ruled by the Suprema in Spain and, although it remained fundamentally the *Spanish* Inquisition, a supreme council was created in Vienna. The Emperor ordered that there should be a very special *auto* to celebrate the change, and this took place at Palermo on 6th April, 1724.

In 1734 Charles III reconquered Sicily, but by this time the Holy Office was past its zenith, and it was in the eighteenth century that it was suppressed.

Lea, quoting Franchina, who was writing in 1744, says that, in less than 300 years, 201 men and women had been burned alive in Sicily on orders from the Holy Office.

## CHAPTER NINE

# SARDINIA

As Sardinia was a dominion of Aragon, the Inquisition was introduced there about the year 1492, with Micer Sancho Maria as Inquisitor. He remained there in this post until 1497 when he was sent to Sicily and was replaced by Gabriel Cardona.

Cardona was soon involved in a quarrel with the Lieutenant-General and Archbishop of Cagliari because he had imprisoned a man – Domingo de Santa Cruz – who they believed should have been left unmolested. The Lieutenant-General and Archbishop, using force, released Santa Cruz, and this was the cause of numerous angry communications between Ferdinand and Sardinia, for Ferdinand was anxious to see the Inquisition supreme over the state.

However it was not long before Cardona was relieved of his post, and the Bishop of Bonavalle took his place. It may have been that Cardona had asked to be allowed to leave Sardinia, for he was certainly in danger of losing his life. The Inquisition was received in Sardinia, as in almost every other country in Europe – certainly by the people, at least – with the utmost suspicion; and Cardona's assistant, Miguel Fonte, who was known as the 'receiver', because it was his duty to deal with confiscated property, had been set upon in Cagliari, and although he had not died immediately and he was taken back to Spain, he very shortly afterwards died of his wounds in Barcelona.

After his assassination it was not easy to find another willing to take the post he had vacated. The dangers of such an unpopular position were fully realized, and it was some months afterwards when Juan López arrived in Sardinia in the role of receiver.

During its early days the Inquisition in Sardinia seemed to

be directed mainly against the *conversos*; but its history is one of disputes and wrangling with the Bishops who, as had happened so many times before, were not pleased to see the authority they had enjoyed pass to the Inquisitors.

Again, as happened before, when the Inquisition moved away from headquarters its officials had a tendency to become more and more corrupt. Unnecessary officials were appointed, and the expenditure was prodigious.

In 1580 Philip II asked Gregory XIII for financial help. This request was not granted. In the reign of Philip III the financial condition of the Inquisition in Sardinia was even more needy. It became difficult to induce people to accept positions in Sardinia, not only on account of the climate but because the remuneration was so small.

In 1718 Sardinia passed into the hands of the Duke of Savoy, and with the cessation of Spanish control the Inquisition ceased to be, and the Bishops resumed the power to condemn people for heresy. The House of Savoy had never taken kindly to the Inquisition, which was a menace to secular power; and as it was a rule of the Church that churchmen could not condemn but must hand over prisoners to the secular arm to be sentenced, persecution for heresy appears to have disappeared in Sardinia during the second half of the eighteenth century.

## CHAPTER TEN

# MILAN

Milan came into Spanish possession in 1529 by the Treaty of Cambrai, and because it became a refuge for those whose opinions differed from the orthodox Catholic Church it received the attention of the Papal Inquisition. But up to the time when it came under Spanish dominion the Inquisition had grown lax. This naturally did not please Philip II who sought to replace the old Inquisition by that more virile version The Spanish Inquisition.

He proposed sending Gaspar Cervantes, who had had a great deal of experience in Spain and who had been made Archbishop of Messina, to begin operations. Cervantes was not eager for the appointment, and the Pope was in no hurry to give his assent.

Meanwhile the people of Milan, hearing what was proposed, became apprehensive – more than that, they began to show that, if any attempt were made to set up the Spanish Inquisition in Milan, they would make trouble.

Philip was eager that there should not be revolt in his possessions and, realizing that the people of Milan had determined not to accept the Spanish Inquisition, he sought to temporize, and made it known to them that he had had no intention of setting up that Inquisition in Milan as it existed in Spain, but had only meant to give them an Inquisitor of experience who would look after them with greater care than they had been accustomed to.

Philip had failed to establish the Spanish Inquisition in Milan. In 1560 Pius IV made his nephew, Cardinal Carlo Borromeo, Archbishop of Milan, a position which gave him power over the whole of Lombardy. The Cardinal went to work with great zeal in the extirpation of heresy, so that it is very doubtful whether, in escaping the Spanish Inquisition, the people of Milan were as lucky as they had believed they would be.

## CHAPTER ELEVEN

# CANARY ISLANDS

In the Canary Islands the Spanish Inquisition was established in 1505 when the Inquisitor-General, Deza, sent Bartolomé López Tribaldos there as Inquisitor (whose power was not great as it was decided that all matters of importance should be referred back to Seville).

At first it languished and was even temporarily suspended, until Espinosa, Inquisitor-General, realizing that by limiting its power it had been crippled, decided to revive it by making it independent of Seville, and appointed the energetic Diego Ortiz de Fúnez to put new life into it.

Fúnez had not been long in the Canaries before he was able to arrange an *auto*. This *auto* attracted such crowds from other islands that the spectators were said to be twice as many as the entire population of Grand Canary. Juan Felipe, one of the victims, who was a Morisco and a rich trader of Lanzarote, discovering that he was about to be arrested, took ship with his family and other *Moriscos* and escaped to Morocco where he was able to give a great deal of information about Inquisitorial methods in the Canaries.

The rule of Fúnez however was soon giving cause for complaint, and a *visitador* was sent out to investigate him. The two became friends and worked together planning *autos*, but at the same time the *visitador* did not hesitate to bring charges against Fúnez. It was the old story. There were so many temptations for these men who had such power and who were far from the centre of authority. Fúnez was accused of allowing Inquisitorial funds to find their way into his own pocket, or carrying on a profitable trade with the Moors of Barbary, of accepting presents; in fact he was accused of all the usual crimes of which a man in his position was likely to be guilty. But returning to Spain he appears to have given a good account of himself at Madrid.

Many English and Dutch sailors were brought before the Tribunal, with many more *conversos* who had escaped to the islands from Spain in the hope of finding a refuge where they could live in peace. *Moriscos* were also persecuted but, strangely enough, there were more cases of blasphemy, sorcery and solicitation in the confessional than of heresy.

There was one case of solicitation which is of particular interest because in this present decade there has been a similar case in France. In 1747 Fray Bartolomé Bello seduced a young girl named Maria Cabral González. Maria became pregnant and a child was born. This the girl took to the priest, her lover, who first baptized it and then strangled it.

As the sentences for solicitation were so light it is not surprising that this crime appears so frequently in the records; and it is only logical to presume that, for every case which came to light, there must have been several which were never heard of, for many women would be very reluctant to come forward and denounce their confessors, particularly if they had submitted. Out of twenty-two men who were brought before the Tribunal in the nineteen months between 1706 and 1708 seven were charged with solicitation (Lea). It is a large proportion.

The Inquisition was suppressed in the Canaries in 1813, and the people were so overjoyed that all the *sanbenitos* which had been hanging in the churches were taken out to the *patios* and publicly burned.

Rejoicing was a little premature, for on 17th August, 1814, a decree was issued which set up the Inquisition again.

But in 1820 it was suppressed for ever, and the Inquisitors left everything and set out for Spain. No respect was paid to the archives, which was a great pity, for they were taken by anyone who cared to do so, with the result that many interesting records are lost to posterity.

## CHAPTER TWELVE

## PORTUGAL

In the year 1580 Portugal was conquered by Philip II, and this meant that its Inquisition came under the zealous eyes of the conqueror. Philip immediately wished to bring the Inquisition of Portugal under the jurisdiction of the Inquisitor-General of Spain, but this the Pope, Gregory XIII, refused to allow; even so, the activities of the Inquisition increased and between 1581 and 1600 fifty *autos de fé* were held.

Now that the two countries were joined under one ruler, many Jews who had been living in Portugal decided to slip into Spain which, as a much richer country, could give them more scope in their enterprises. Ninety thousand of them had taken refuge in Portugal after the exodus of 1492. John II had allowed them to stay on payment of large sums of money, but their stay was to have been temporary. Many Jews however had become Christians in order to be allowed to remain; and it was these people who now returned to Spain.

By the end of the sixteenth century, after some twenty years of Spanish domination, Portugal had become very impoverished. Rich merchants had left Lisbon, so that the once busy city was almost deserted; only 200 remained of the country's 700 ships, and the harvests were poor. The people blamed the Jews for this. Early in the century, at Easter 1506, the terrible Lisbon massacre had taken place – that rising against the Jews which continued for three days and nights and in which several thousands lost their lives.

The Inquisition of Portugal was even more notorious for its cruelty than that of Spain, but there was one man who, in the seventeenth century, sought to make reforms. This was Antonio Vieyra, a Jesuit, who came back to Portugal from South America in the year 1661 and was shocked by what he saw.

He was brought up in Bahia and educated at the Jesuit

school, and although his parents (according to Rule, who refers to the Jesuits as 'an ill-reputed company') did not intend him to become a Jesuit he was weaned from his parents by the Society.

When he was thirty-three John IV gave him a position as preacher in the chapel-royal; and because he was exceptionally brilliant, and the King presumably felt that he was wasted merely as a preacher, he was sent on certain diplomatic missions and in this capacity did the King's work in Holland, France, England, and Rome.

He then became a missionary and went to Brazil, but after a while the Portuguese authorities there decided to expel the Jesuit missionaries, and Vieyra returned to Lisbon where he was given a post at Court. He had his enemies in Lisbon and was forced to leave for Coimbra; but not content with his banishment these enemies sought to destroy him, and the simplest way of doing this was to bring a charge of heresy against him.

His sermons were noted and everything he said was sifted for a sentence that could be called heretical.

By October 1665 he was in the prison of the Inquisition.

It was held against him that he condemned examination of heresies and had declared that it would be well for the kingdom if the names of informers and witnesses were made known to the New Christians who were accused of Judaism. He had also expressed the desire that Jews should be allowed to take public offices, and that, provided they did not attack Christians, they should be allowed to worship as they pleased.

He had also expressed sympathy for the victims of the Inquisition and had published writings concerning their sufferings.

He had recorded the case of a certain Maria dá Conceiçâo who had been arrested by the Inquisition on a charge of Judaizing. She had been put on the rack and, after she had been cruelly treated there, she finally 'confessed' as the torturers wished her to; when she was able to use her limbs she was taken before the examiners and asked to ratify her confession. Very boldly she spoke up. Torture had driven her to say what she did not mean; she retracted her confession. She was again tortured, again confessed, and later again refused to confirm what she had said on the rack. She told the Inquisitors that, even though under torture she had said what they demanded of her, as soon as she was taken from the torture chamber she would tell the truth. She was racked a third time, and this time she did not confess.

The furious Inquisitors condemned her to be whipped through the streets of Lisbon and then to be banished to the west coast of Africa.

Vieyra had also written vivid descriptions of the prisons of the Inquisition in which he states it was customary to put five people in a cell nine feet by eleven, and in which the vessels were only changed once a week, and the only light and air which penetrated this foul place came through a narrow slit in the ceiling.

Such a man was dangerous to the Inquisition, but he was a highly-respected member of the Society of Jesus; therefore the Inquisition could not treat him as they would some poor *Marrano, Morisco* or Protestant far from home.

His sentence was that he should be deprived of the authority to preach and sent to a college or house of Jesuits which the Holy Office would select; he should be unable to leave this particular college without first obtaining the consent of the Inquisition.

It was decided that he should be taken to the Jesuit House at Perroso which had been chosen for him, but the decision was changed and he was sent to the house of the Cotovia in Lisbon.

About this time the Jesuits were instrumental in helping the Queen Mother, Doña Luisa, to depose Alfonso VI and set Pedro IV on the throne, so the Jesuits were in high favour with the new king. Vieyra was released, and left Lisbon for Rome.

From Rome he made an attack on the Inquisition; he wrote that the Portuguese Inquisition had become a tribunal which robbed men of their fortunes and their lives and could not tell the difference between guilt and innocence, that while it proclaimed its piety, it was guilty of injustice and cruelty.

This was very heartening to the New Christians who had great hopes of bringing the Inquisition in Portugal more in line with that of Rome.

In 1671 there was a general attack on the New Christians in Lisbon. The trouble started when it was stated that some wafers had been stolen from a church. This may have been falsely rumoured and the wafers may not have been stolen at all. However, the Inquisitors decided to use the occasion for a fresh attack on the New Christians.

They were arrested in hundreds and submitted to the most cruel forms of torture. But the people were becoming more enlightened as time was passing; many of the more educated were horrified at what was happening, and made a petition to the King imploring him to stop this wave of terror.

The King, too much in awe of the Inquisition even at this date to interfere, did refer the matter to Rome. Meanwhile the thief was discovered not to be a New Christian but an old one. But the Inquisitors would not release their prisoners, and stated that they meant to hold them for further questioning.

Pope Clement X asked the Inquisitors to send him records of a few trials so that he might judge the manner in which they were conducted. They had to be threatened with excommunication before they would forward two cases.

The King then asked the Pope to study the rules of the Inquisition as it was carried out in Portugal, and make reforms. Nothing was gained however. It was difficult to act from a distance and the Inquisitors were at this stage very powerful. Yet there must have been a certain comfort, to those living in constant fear, to know that people – in high places – were concerned to win justice for them.

## CHAPTER THIRTEEN

# GOA

It was St Francis Xavier who urged the King of Portugal to set up the Inquisition in the Portuguese possession of Goa. He had noticed that 'Jewish perfidy' was daily spreading in the countries of east India which were subject to the crown of Portugal, and implored the King to set up the Holy Office there as the only remedy. Thus he wrote in November 1545.

When Portugal had taken possession of Goa in 1510, a bishopric had been established and the usual methods of converting the population were applied. Children were taken from their parents and brought up as Catholics, and there were many forcible baptisms.

Although St Francis Xavier's plea was not answered, by 1560 Aleixo Diaz Falcão was sent to Goa as Inquisitor, and the tribunal he formed became known as one of the most merciless in the Christian world.

To repeat the processes of establishment and to give accounts of procedure would become boring because they were much the same as in other instances; I think though that the best pictures of the Inquisition come from those people who actually experienced it and lived to tell the tale.

We have a good picture of the Inquisition of Goa from the Frenchman, Monsieur Dellon, who wrote his own account of his adventures in his book *Relation de L'Inquisition de Goa* (Paris 1688).

Monsieur Dellon, a traveller in India, was staying for a time at Damaun on the north-west coast of Hindustan. He was paying attention to a certain woman, but unfortunately for him the governor of the place and a priest had designs on the same woman. Presumably French gallantries were about to succeed, and this so angered the other two suitors that they decided to do something about it.

Dellon had been careless in his conversation. No doubt he thought that as a Frenchman he had nothing to fear from the Inquisition (this happened in the 1670s) and he had freely stated his scorn for some Catholic beliefs.

The priest happened to be secretary of the Inquisition at Damaun; so that it was not difficult for the two unsuccessful suitors to conspire together to get Dellon arrested.

To the Frenchman's surprise and dismay he was seized one night and conveyed to a prison where he was forced to exist with the lowest possible criminals; and here he was left for four months.

At the end of that time he was put into irons and taken aboard ship, which stopped at Bacaim for a short stay, during which they were lodged in noisome prisons and then taken on to Goa.

The Archbishop arranged that the prisoners should be kept in his own prison until they could be taken to that of the Inquisition. Dellon wrote of it that it was the most filthy, dark and horrible he ever saw, and he doubted whether there was a prison more shocking anywhere. It was a kind of cave in which there was no light but that which came through a little hole, and the stench was terrible.

Eventually he was loaded with irons and taken to the Prison of the Inquisition. There his irons were taken off and he was at length summoned to an audience.

In the room which was known as the Board of the Holy Office sat the Grand Inquisitor of the Indies at the end of a huge table which was set upon a dais. This was in the centre of the room, and at the end of it was a large cross which reached almost from floor to ceiling. Close to the crucifix a notary was seated on a stool.

Dellon was asked by the Inquisitor whether he knew why he had been arrested, and he told his story, to which the Inquisitor, Francisco Delgado Ematos, listened. Then he rang a bell and the prisoner was taken away and stripped of all his possessions. His hair was cropped to his head. His imprisonment in the Holy House had begun.

He gives us a good description of the institution in Goa during the seventeenth century, and wrote that the building was large and grand, that there were three gates in front and that prisoners entered by the central one, when they mounted a great staircase and entered the hall. The servants of the Inquisition used the side gates which led to their apartments in the building. There was another building at the rear of the main one and in this were the cells, which opened into galleries. The lower-floor cells were tiny and there was no way of letting in the light, while the upper cells were much more comfortable, being high and vaulted, each having a small window.

The prisoners were each given an earthen pot in which to wash, and another pot for other purposes which was emptied once in four days. They had three meals a day and there were doctors on the premises to attend to the sick. Any who died were unceremoniously buried in the precincts of the building, and if they were considered to be guilty of heresy their bones would be dug up to be burned at the next *auto de fé*.

Any prisoner who spoke, groaned, or even sighed was immediately and severely beaten.

Every two months an Inquisitor and notary visited the prisoner to ask if he was being well looked after. It was wise to answer in the affirmative. Dellon had been told that if he desired an audience he had only to ask for it; yet again and again he implored that he might be given one. This was the formality of the Inquisition which was the same at Goa as in Spain or Portugal.

At length he obtained his audience, was once more asked if he knew the reason of his arrest, and repeated what he believed he had said at Damaun. The Inquisitor replied that he had been wise to accuse himself, and asked him in the name of Jesus Christ to complete his self-accusation that he might reap the benefit of the tenderness and mercy which the Tribunal always showed towards those who confessed without being forced to do so.

These were ominous words and meant to strike terror into the heart of the prisoner; and after they had been delivered Dellon was taken back to his cell to brood on them.

After a fortnight there was another audience when he was again asked if he knew the reason for his arrest. He was then told to repeat the Paternoster, Hail Mary, the Creed and Commandments of God, the Commandments of the Church and *Salve Regina*. All this Dellon was able to do in such a manner that even they could find no fault with it. Then came the warning: In the name of Jesus Christ he must confess more.

Fearing what was in store, Dellon tried to commit suicide by starvation. Finding this unsuccessful he invented more confessions and asked for another audience. But what he had to tell was not enough and he was sent back to his cell once more.

He pretended to be ill and a doctor ordered that he be bled. He tore off the bandages hoping to bleed to death; but again he was unsuccessful.

The priest who had been sent to confess him was a kindly Franciscan, and when Dellon confided his terrors to him, the monk arranged that he should have a companion in his cell. As a result a Negro, who was in prison on a charge of sorcery, was sent to keep him company, and life became more tolerable, but eventually the Negro was removed.

Once more he attempted to commit suicide, was discovered by his jailers, and his life saved. After this he was put into irons, but so desperate did he become that he threw himself about in a frenzy and it was necessary to take off his irons to prevent him from doing himself further injury.

He saw men and women taken past his cell to and from the torture chambers; he heard their groans, saw them bloodstained and crippled. Presumably this was a form of mental torture, a reminder that this fate was probably in store for *him*.

One Sunday in January 1676, when he offered his dirty linen to the jailer to be washed, he was alarmed to hear the jailer say that he did not want it. He then heard the bells ringing and, guessing that there would be an *auto de fé* next day, was convinced that he would be taken to the stake and burned to death.

The next morning a vest and a pair of trousers were brought to him, and barefoot he was taken from his cell to a large hall, lit only by a few lamps and ominously gloomy, where he found other prisoners – about 200 in all – and they were all commanded to sit in a gallery.

Among one section of the prisoners priests moved; quite clearly they were urging these miserable people to confess and become reconciled to the Church that they might receive the 'mercy' of strangulation before the flames consumed their bodies.

Dellon had been taken to this room at two o'clock in the morning and after he had been there for two hours refreshment was offered in the form of bread and figs. When Dellon, who had rarely felt less like eating, refused the food, he was advised to take it and put it in his pocket for he would be hungry before he returned.

The last phrase seemed to him revealing and he guessed that he was not destined to suffer at the stake that day.

Immediately before dawn the cathedral bell began to toll and the people crowded into the streets as the prisoners were led out.

They were marched to the Church of St Francis and by the time they arrived Dellon's feet were sore and bleeding from the flinty stones which had been scattered about to cause suffering to the barefooted prisoners. As the heat was intense, the *auto* was not to be celebrated out of doors but to take place in the church.

There the Grand Inquisitor and the Viceroy were seated in state and on the altar was the crucifix between huge silver candlesticks.

The sermon was preached by the Provincial of the Augustinians and Dellon has noted his comparison of the Inquisition with Noah's Ark which, said the preacher, received all sorts of wild beasts and sent them out tame.

The crimes of each prisoner were enumerated and the sentences read. Dellon's crimes were that he had doubted whether images should be adored and had referred to an ivory crucifix as a piece of ivory. He had criticized the Inquisition and spoken of it with contempt; he had maintained the invalidity of baptism and he was accused of 'ill intention' towards the Faith. For these crimes he was to lose all his property; he was to be banished from India and to serve five years in the Portuguese galleys with additional penances which the Inquisitors would decide upon.

There were two people of whom the Inquisition had washed its hands, and these two – a man and a woman – were to be taken out to the *quemadero*, the Campo Santa Lazaro near the river, to be burned, together with effigies of some prisoners who had died.

Dellon was taken to Lisbon where he was put to work with convicts; eventually some of his own countrymen secured his release.

Rule gives an account of how an English Anglican cleric, Dr Claudius Buchanan, visited Goa in the year 1808, and much to his surprise was entertained by Friar Joseph à Doloribus who was an Inquisitor of high standing in the Tribunal.

By this time the Inquisition was far less powerful than it had been in the days when Dellon had been its victim, and *autos de fé* were no longer held in public, sentences being carried out within the walls of the prison.

Dr Buchanan, who was a writer as well as a priest, accepted the hospitality offered by the Inquisitor, for he believed that he might discover, through him, something of the secret working of the Inquisition, which he could make known to the world.

Friar Joseph, refusing to acknowledge the Anglican orders of his visitor, expressed his interest in his literary work; but Dr Buchanan insisted on discussing the Inquisition. He gave the Inquisitor Dellon's book, *Relation de l'Inquisition de Goa*, which had been translated into Portuguese. When Friar Joseph had read the book he declared it to be quite untrue, but Dr Buchanan was not to be put off so easily, and he asked Friar Joseph to mark the passages which were lies; and he told the Inquisitor that he had other books in his possession which confirmed Dellons' statements.

Friar Joseph eventually admitted that Dellon's descriptions of the prison were true, but that he had misunderstood the motives of the Inquisition and had written without charity of Holy Church.

Dr Buchanan then made a request. Could he not see the building of the Inquisition? He was writing a book about India, and he could not do this adequately without some reference to the Inquisition. Perhaps there was a slight threat in the doctor's words. Perhaps he implied: If I am not allowed to see what I want, I must presume that there is some reason for keeping it from me. British prestige in India was high, and the Inquisitor was in a quandary. Reluctantly he agreed to show his guest the building of the Inquisition.

Dr Buchanan was accordingly taken to the great hall which had been described by Dellon, and there he met several of the officials and familiars who, he thought, seemed silent, severe, and embarrassed.

When he had examined the hall he asked to see the dungeons and the prisoners. That could not be, he was told. But, declared Dr Buchanan, unless he saw the prisoners he would be obliged to believe that Dellon's descriptions were true, and that the Inquisitors were hiding something. If prisoners were treated well, as Friar Joseph suggested, would it not be wise to let a writer see them, that he might explain this to the world? He wanted to see the two hundred dungeons which were ten feet square, and which had been described by those men who had been imprisoned in them and lived to describe them. Dr Buchanan added ominously that he wished to see if there were any British subjects among them for whom it might be his duty to seek protection. He wanted to see the torture chambers and to discover what method of punishment was used within the secret prison to replace that of the *auto de fé*. And, added the doctor, if he were not allowed to discover these things, naturally he must presume the worst.

The Inquisitor had nothing to say, and intimated that he had no more time to spare for Dr Buchanan.

Dr Buchanan then thanked him for his hospitality, and begged him to answer one question. This was: How many prisoners were there in the cells? The Inquisitor replied that it was a question he could not answer.

In 1774 the Tribunal was abolished and re-established in 1779, and in 1812, when Dr Buchanan's *Christian Researches in Asia* appeared, it was still in existence; but it was finally suppressed in 1812.

## CHAPTER FOURTEEN

# OLIVARES

With the coming of the Bourbon dynasty to Spain it was inevitable that the Inquisition should slide down that swift decline to eventual impotence. Louis XIV had summed up his attitude in the famous words '*L'état c'est moi*'.

This was the Bourbon policy; and the Bourbon Kings of Spain intended that it should apply in Spain as in France; and as the Inquisition was an institution which had for so long proved itself to be even more powerful than the state it must be reduced to second place.

It seems extraordinary that the country which had once been the richest in the world should have made such a rapid decline, that it should have been ready to accept the Bourbons, and that the Inquisition, which by its secret methods had amassed such power, should have begun its slow recession.

But a glance at the history of the country, from the end of the reign of the second Philip to the end of that of the fourth, will give an idea of how this state of affairs came about.

The character of Philip II has been frequently examined in these pages; and when on his death-bed he contemplated the coming reign with apprehension and said of his son Philip that he feared his favourites would rule him, Philip's foresight had not deceived him.

Philip II had had a simple faith. As long as he could satisfy his conscience he was at peace; if the results of his actions were disastrous, in his absolute belief in divine control, he could say, 'That is the will of God.' Perhaps this was a reason why, in the battle of wits with Elizabeth I, he was the loser.

Philip III was not a fool but he was weak and, as his father had prophesied, in the hands of his favourites. Because of his weakness it was natural that the Inquisition should become even more powerful; but the times were changing, the people were becoming more enlightened, as was inevitable with the passing of time. As the Inquisition grew more powerful, so the nation appeared to be more devout – it had to do so to avoid the attention of the Inquisitors. Yet it was a surface devoutness, a matter of expediency; and the awakening to reality was beginning to set in.

Under Philip III the prosperity of the nation declined. The people were starving; the cloth-weaving industry was being ruined by the *alcabala*; the King's chief minister and favourite, the Duke of Lerma, had tampered with the currency; and all the time such extravagance was maintained at the Court as had never been indulged in during the reign of Philip II.

On the day when Philip IV was born the *Moriscos* had staged their rising; the King had discovered that they were guilty of plotting against Spain with Henry IV of France, with the Duke of Savoy, Elizabeth I, and with the King of Fez. They had been expelled from the country with the result that an industrious section of the population had been lost, the farmlands had become derelict and the irrigation system was no longer working.

In spite of signs of ruin, the King continued in his extravagant policy; and the people were taxed still further to pay for the lavish ceremonies in which the favourites delighted; and the King sought to ease his conscience by building convents.

But Philip III was not entirely stupid and was fully aware of the state to which the country was reduced. Early in 1619 he caused reports to be drawn up that he might have full understanding of the poverty which had overtaken his people; the results shocked him so profoundly that he called a halt to extravagance. He was not yet forty but he had little desire for life. He was clever enough to know that his rule had brought Spain to the state to which she had come. His great concern was to repent in time, that his soul might be saved; and to show that his repentance was genuine he sought to instil into his son the need to govern with wisdom and make a better job of kingship than his father had.

The favourites who had circulated about Philip III were aware of his delicate state of health, which was not helped by the remorse which had now come to him.

They considered the heir who, it seemed to them, would soon mount the throne and look for favourites of his own; the Duke of Lerma's enemies sought to place new favourites about the Infante, and one of these was Gaspar de Guzman, Count of Olivares, a young man of twenty-eight.

Olivares became a gentleman of the chamber to the Infante, and immediately began to exert a great influence over him. Philip, not yet fourteen, pale and sandy haired, was in awe of the handsome, domineering Olivares who began to form the boy's character as he wished it to be. At first young Philip had been a little resentful of Olivares, but the Count soon won the boy's respect and friendship, and then proceeded to arrange his household.

Olivares chose the Infante's servants who were all his own supporters; talked to the boy about the affairs of the country and instilled in him a desire to rule with greater success than his father had; and in every way prepared to become the power behind the throne on the death of Philip III, which it was clear at this stage could not be long delayed.

In 1612 the King's eldest daughter Ana was betrothed to Louis XIII of France, and the young Infante Philip to Isabel of Bourbon, eldest daughter of Henri Quatre.

The ceremonies that attended these betrothals and the entry of Isabel into Spain were extravagant in the extreme. In July 1619 the King and his son made a ceremonial visit to Portugal where the young fourteen-year-old boy, magnificent in white satin covered with gold and jewels and in black velvet shoulder cape, received the homage of the Portuguese who took their oaths to accept him as their ruler on the death of his father; then he in turn took his oath that he would respect their rights.

On this journey Olivares accompanied his Prince, for it was believed that the King's low state of health might prevent his ever returning to Madrid.

In November 1620, Olivares, who had encouraged the Infante in sexual adventure, decided that the married life of the boy and his young bride should commence; at this time Philip was fifteen and a half, and the couple started married life in the palace of Pardo under the eyes of Olivares.

Meanwhile the King's health was deteriorating rapidly and,

although he occasionally made slight recovery, he was close to death. He was full of remorse for what he conceived to be an evil life since he was convinced that he had been an unworthy ruler; and he was hysterical, imploring his confessors to plead on his account with the saints; he was terrified of death; and on one occasion when he was very ill indeed the dead body of Saint Isadore of Madrid was brought to him that he might hold the corpse in his arms. When this was done and the King's health improved, all were sure that this was due to the presence of the dead body in his bed; but a few months after that brief recovery he was dying and this time nothing could save him.

Terrified of the vengeance which he felt would be waiting for him on his death, he sent for his son – now sixteen years old. He implored him to learn his lesson from his father's life; above all things he begged him to keep Spain absolutely Catholic and see that his sister Maria made a Catholic alliance (Charles, Prince of Wales, afterwards the ill-fated Charles I, was angling for Maria at this time).

This was the hour for which Olivares had been waiting. His young Infante was now Philip IV.

The new King was of a generous nature and kindly; in his youth he was less devoted to religion than his father had been and more fond of sensual pleasures. In public he conducted himself with the solemnity demanded of Spanish monarchs, but in private he was very gay and even witty; and the friends whose company he most delighted in were writers, actors, musicians and painters. He was later to become one of the greatest royal patrons of art.

His sensuality however governed all his feelings and he was unable to escape from it; and as he, like his father, was troubled by a conscience, he would suffer greatly after those debauches which, at the time he indulged in them, he was unable to resist.

His wife, Isabel, was charming and pretty, and Philip was delighted with her; but this did not prevent his continuing with ex-marital love affairs, for this indulgence, even at his early age, had become a habit. As for Isabel, she was the daughter of Marie de'Medici and the gallant Henri Quatre who has been said to have had more mistresses than any other king of France, even including François Premier. There was the inevitable scandal; and, although Philip found it impossible to be a faithful husband, he was very jealous of his wife.

It was very shortly after the wedding that the King showed his jealousy in the well-known incident concerning Don Juan de Tassis, the Count of Villa Mediana. It will be remembered that the Count was reputed to have ridden into the arena, during the jousts, his device being a mass of those silver coins known as *reals* (or royals). Above them were inscribed the words *My loves are*— His ardent glances were directed towards the Queen and the meaning read into his actions was that he was attempting to win her favours. This was probably deliberately meant to discountenance the young King, because at that time Villa Mediana was seeking to win the affection of Francisca de Tavara who was one of Philip's mistresses.

He succeeded, however, in annoying the King, and the Queen did not help when she murmured to the King that Villa Mediana aimed well. Philip is reputed to have snapped ominously: 'Yes – and he aims too high!'

A few months later another scene took place in which the gallant Count played a prominent part. Philip was enamoured of the play and Isabel shared his enthusiasm. To celebrate the King's seventeenth birthday a tent theatre was erected outdoors and the comedy *La Gloria de Niquea* was to be played for his entertainment, Queen Isabel herself taking a part.

During the play the stage curtain caught fire and Philip hastened to the back of the tent to see if Isabel were safe. The tent by that time was ablaze and, when Philip came upon his wife, he found her half fainting in the arms of Villa Mediana.

The gossips declared that the bold Count had staged the fire so that he might gallantly rescue the Queen.

These stories are said to be fabrications of over-imaginative writers, and historian Martin Hume is careful to state that some of them depend on the 'untrustworthy evidence' of the French writer Madame d'Aulnoy; but there is no doubt that the final scene in the drama did take place.

Four months after the burning of the tent, one night when Villa Mediana was driving home, his coach passed under the arch of the Calle Mayor and as it did so a masked figure appeared and shot a bolt from a cross-bow at him. The aim was very accurate and Villa Mediana was pierced through the heart. Villa Mediana staggered out of the coach and was drawing his sword when he fell dying on the cobbles.

The King was suspected of having instigated this murder.

Both Philip and Isabel shared a love of pleasure. Philip would rise in the morning to find Olivares at his side instructing him in the affairs which had to be attended to that day; he was only too delighted to leave them in the hands of this man who, many said, was the true king of Spain.

If Philip and his Queen were fond of lavish spectacles and encouraged the theatre, they never forgot their duty to the Catholic Church and many of the spectacles they arranged, or which were arranged for them, were religious ceremonies.

This was an atmosphere in which the Inquisition flourished.

The first child, a princess, had been prematurely born in 1621, and had died; and the second, Margarita Maria, died a month after her birth; but before that, a lavish ceremony had been arranged to celebrate her birth and baptism.

The hysterical atmosphere of devotion will be understood when the affair of Reynard de Peralta is recalled.

This French pedlar wandered into the church of the Augustinian Monastery of St Philip at that time when it was crowded with sightseers and worshippers who had come to give thanks for the birth of the baby Infanta.

Imagine Madrid at this time of celebration. The excitement would be intense, the bells ringing, the crowds jostling each other in the streets and particularly in the *Mentidero* (Liars' Walk where actors, authors and those down on their luck assembled to exchange and recite satirical verse about the Court.) At noon the angelus would call the hungry writers and their friends who would assemble at the gates of the monastery where bread and soup were given them; eagerly they would eat and talk endlessly of the hope the young King had given men of their profession.

And suddenly Reynard de Peralta walked into the church and made his gesture. He knelt at the altar and we are told that he insulted the Holy Mystery, which was tantamount to a denial of the Immaculate Conception.

Peralta was seized and dragged before the Tribunal of the Inquisition.

There was only one end for such a man; he was found guilty of heresy and handed to the secular arm for punishment. He repented in time and was reconciled, thus earning the mercy of strangulation before his body was burned.

But the hysteria which ran through Madrid after this event gives an indication as to why the Inquisition was in full flower.

The Church had been defiled, and Madrid was plunged in mourning on this account. More ceremonies were hastily devised, not brilliant, colourful displays, but processions marched through the streets carrying the cross draped in black crêpe; and in these processions walked men and women, bare-backed, flagellating themselves and each other, presumably in the hope of placating the Virgin Mary for the insult which had been paid to her by the heretic pedlar.

The churches were hung with black crêpe and for a whole week no plays were to be performed, and prostitutes were forbidden to ply their trade.

Madrid gave itself up to this religious hysteria during that week which was to have been devoted to festivity.

This was characteristic; side by side with profligacy and wanton extravagance was this ostentatious piety.

Two theatres had been built in Madrid; they were not in the least like the theatres which were to flourish in London under Charles II. They were situated in courtyards surrounded by houses; and the houses belonged to the owners of the theatre and formed part of it. At one end of the courtyard was a stage covered by tiled eaves; and there was an awning over the seats which were set up in the courtyard. Men occupied these seats, and the women used an enclosed space, not unlike a gallery, on the cobbles, which was given the name of *cazuela* (stewpan). In the houses, watching from the windows were the nobility. These two theatres became notorious for the intrigues which were carried on in the houses, where the most adventurous had all the opportunities they sought.

The Queen was very gay and often, to amuse her, fights

would be started among the common people in the courtyard seats, and there was one occasion, so it is reported, when snakes were let loose in one of these courtyards so that the Queen could be amused by the panic of the people.

But the most exciting spectacle of all to the people of this time was the *auto de fé*, and the Inquisition was ready to provide the people with the amusement they demanded.

Philip and Isabel were present at the *auto* of 4th July, 1624; and because of this almost the whole Court attended also. Balconies had to be fitted up and hung with silks and velvet; and a special stage was erected. Because this was a royal occasion the stage was crowded with high officials of the Supreme Council, as well as those from the Inquisition of Toledo and the Town Council of Madrid.

The evening before the day of the *auto* the procession left the Convent of Doña Maria de Aragon carrying the great green cross in accordance with the usual custom, but on this day the bearer of the cross was the Constable of Castile, and the Admiral of Castile was entrusted with the tassels of the banner.

Early next morning Philip and Isabel left the palace with the Court for the balconies, and as soon as they were seated the procession began.

Many of the victims on this occasion were Jews who, it was said, had been in the habit of meeting in a house in the Calle de las Infantas in order to practise the rites of the Law of Moses and to insult Christians by flogging a crucifix.

The Inquisitor-General administered the oath to Philip to keep the purity of the Church inviolate at no matter what cost; and this oath was afterwards repeated by the members of the council. The King's confessor preached his sermon, the sentences were read; and at three o'clock in the afternoon, when all these ceremonies were concluded, the prisoners were led to their punishment — seven of them condemned to be burned alive in the *quemadero*.

There can be little doubt that while Philip and his Queen proved their devotion to the Church by showing themselves at scenes like this, they believed that they were expiating their sins, and since they could be so pious their little frivolities were of no account.

This was the spirit in which the Inquisition flourished; and the nation followed the example set by the Court.

Olivares was determined to lead the King. No one was allowed to enter the royal bedchamber before he did; he himself drew the curtains and stood beside the King whilst he dressed, never allowing Philip to put on a garment which had not passed through his hands.

He was nearly twenty years older than Philip and Philip took his advice on all matters. Olivares was not a man who was out to gain wealth and power merely for his own gratification; he wished to make the country strong and if his policies eventually failed it was because of a lack of unity in Spain. The Aragonese stood aloof, as did the Catalans; as though they had been separate states. Portugal was a conquered country and had never given real allegiance to Spain. Such a lack of unity brought Olivares, good statesman though he was, face to face with insurmountable difficulties which were eventually to give his enemies the chance they needed.

He was determined that he and he alone should lead the King, and each morning when he entered the royal bedchamber to draw the curtains, his pockets would be stuffed with state papers, and documents would even be stuck in the band of his hat, which caused a great deal of amusement to the Court who wondered how the pleasure-loving King could tolerate such a reminder of business at an early hour in the morning when he was sleeping off the effects of last night's junketings.

However, Olivares remained supreme in those early years of the reign, and his power even over the Inquisition is apparent in the rather comic affair of the *Golilla*.

During the reign of Philip III enormous ruffs had become fashionable. Some of these were quite ridiculous, and efforts had been made to change the fashion and to bring back the Walloon collar into general use. This flat collar which fell on to the shoulders was very plain after the glorious ruffs, and the people rejected it; their grounds for doing so were that it was greatly favoured by the Flemings and therefore the collar was connected with heresy in the minds of the people.

Then a tailor of the Calle Mayor invented a new collar. This was made of cardboard which was covered with cloth to match the doublet and lined with silk. Heated irons and shellac applied to the cardboard enabled the tailor to make it into a most graceful shape which bent outwards where it reached the chin and showed the beautiful silk lining.

When he had completed the collar the tailor took it to the King, who was delighted with it; and the tailor considering this patronage from the King, believed he had made his fortune with the *Golilla*, which was the name given to the new collar. No doubt the tailor had his rivals – those makers of ruffs and Walloons – who realized that his success would mean their failure, and it was very easy to trump up a charge against him. How did he achieve that wondrous sweeping curve? He had some devilish machine for doing it, and it was sorcery because, it was said, while the irons were applied he must mutter incantations to his master, the Devil.

Very soon someone had informed the Inquisition, and the tailor was brought before the Tribunal, on a charge of sorcery. The Inquisition ordered that all the goods should be taken from his shop and burned before his door.

Fortunately for the tailor he had supplied the collars to the King, and he sent frantic messages to Olivares begging his help.

Olivares, who no doubt had decided to adopt the *Golilla* which did not have to be washed and lasted for about a year, was annoyed; he summoned the Inquisitors to his presence, jeered at their stupidity and ordered the immediate release of the tailor.

As the tailor was released and allowed to continue making collars, it is clear that Olivares was the most powerful man in Spain. In a very short time *Golillas* were being generally worn there and in other countries; in France they were less popular, the French considering them somewhat inelegant and inventing the jabot and the lace cravat to replace them.

In 1634, when the finances of Spain were very low indeed, Olivares began negotiations with Jews in the Levant and Africa, and granted licences for certain of them to return to Spain. He explained that they should have a district in Madrid assigned to them, for he believed that they could bring financial prosperity back to the country.

Again he shows how powerful was his position, since he dared make such a suggestion; but, touched on such a vulnerable spot, the Inquisition roused itself and demanded the dismissal of Olivares, for, it was said, if such a man were allowed to make his wild dreams actualities, the Faith of Spain would be ruined.

Philip, under the sway of Olivares as he was, was nevertheless subservient to the Inquisition; like his father he was from time to time worried by his conscience and feared what was waiting for him on the other side of death.

This time the Inquisition won, regarding the Jews.

On another occasion Olivares demanded to see records of certain cases with which the Inquisition was dealing. This the Inquisitor-General, at this time Sotomayor, refused to allow; but Olivares became threatening and Sotomayor was forced to comply. Sotomayor melodramatically laid the papers at the foot of a crucifix, hoping to appeal to the superstition in Olivares. But Olivares was unimpressed by such gestures; he seized the papers, burned them and freed the prisoners whom they concerned.

It was said that one of Olivares's projects was to abolish the Inquisition altogether, and that he would seize an opportunity of advising the King to this course. But Philip was the kind of man who clung to religion; to indulge in religious ceremonies, after an extravagant debauch, comforted him. He felt that whatever the state of Spain, she was still a Catholic country. He would never have consented to the abolition of the Inquisition, the iron rule of which kept the country Catholic.

The Inquisition, naturally, did not forget the man who had done so much to perturb it.

Olivares had his worries. In 1627 Philip fell ill and it was believed that he could not live. His baby daughter had died and the Queen was pregnant, but Olivares was uncertain of the Queen's ability to bear a child who would live. Carlos, the elder of the King's two brothers (the other, Fernando, had been made a cardinal), was no friend of Olivares.

While the King lay in this desperate state, his bedchamber full of old bones and other relics which had been brought in the hope of saving him, plots were going on to oust Olivares from his position.

But this time the King recovered and Olivares had the pleasure of discomfiting his enemies.

Philip's conscience troubled him greatly at such times. He was worried about the life he had led. He had had thirty illegitimate children – perhaps more – and some of these had received great honours. The most favoured was Don John of Austria, a very handsome boy on whom Philip doted, for, as happened so often in royal houses, while he failed to get a legitimate heir, his bastards were healthy and handsome – and Don John was the healthiest and most handsome of them all.

Moreover Philip had been deeply in love with the boy's mother, Maria Calderon, who was a sixteen-year-old actress when Philip first saw her. The King, watching her from the *aposento* (one of those rooms of the houses which looked on the courtyard of the theatre) decided to make her his mistress. Maria was a very virtuous girl, and remained faithful to the King; she looked forward to the day when the King should cease to desire her, for it was a custom that a king's mistress should have no other lover and that when the affair was over she should retire to a convent. When Don John was born, Maria begged to be allowed to go into a convent; and Philip, who was deeply in love with her, tried to dissuade her from this; but eventually he gave way to her pleadings, made her an abbess, and remained devoted to her son.

In October 1629, six months after the birth of Don John, Philip's legitimate son was born: Baltasar Carlos, Infante of Spain and heir to the throne.

Olivares had succeeded in winning the enmity of the Queen, for, since he undertook to pander to the King's pleasures, this was almost inevitable. Moreover, he excluded her from political matters. Therefore, while continuing in the King's good graces, the minister was accumulating a large number of enemies in high places, and the Queen's position was strengthened as young Baltasar Carlos appeared to be growing into a healthy boy.

A quarrel arose between the Inquisition and the judges of the

Court; and some minor officials on both sides were imprisoned by the authorities on the opposing side. Lawlessness broke out in the capital and there was war with France. Everything that went wrong was blamed on Olivares.

But Olivares was still strong; and when the nobleman, Lujanes, made a scene in the royal chapel by kneeling before the King and imploring him to rid himself of Olivares, although poor Lujanes was declared to be mad he was imprisoned and when he died mysteriously a few days later it was generally believed that the minister had arranged for him to be poisoned.

Lujanes was not the only one who protested against the minister; the people in the streets cried out that he must go.

Olivares gained more enemies when he brought to the Court a young man of twenty-eight whom he acknowledged as his son. This young man was now known as Enrique Felipe de Guzman, and previously had been brought up by a Madrid government official. Enrique Felipe was by no means attractive, and was in fact somewhat crude in manners; before he had been brought to Court and acknowledged by Olivares, he had married, but this was declared invalid as Olivares wanted a grander marriage for his son. Philip was induced to bestow honours upon him, and Olivares demanded for him the daughter of the Duke of Frias, Constable of Castile – and the Duke agreed to the demand, being afraid to do otherwise.

But although he was still master at Court, the people were murmuring against Olivares. He needed money to face the French; the Portuguese had escaped from Spanish domination; the currency had been debased; many people were in prisons in Madrid because they had either refused to pay or could not pay the taxes demanded of them; and for all these misfortunes the people blamed Olivares. They said that he had advised the King to legitimize Don John of Austria, merely because he wished to bring his own illegitimate son to Court and have him legitimized.

Olivares now had too many powerful enemies; the Queen, his rivals at Court, the people and the Inquisition.

The Spanish on sea and land were beaten and the French were already on Spanish soil. Philip roused himself from his pleasure-loving existence and determined to put himself at the head of his troops. Olivares opposed this, but Philip, at last, decided to act against the advice of the minister who had dominated him so long. The Queen became Regent and Olivares was no favourite of the Queen. He joined the King but he was beginning to see that his hold on the monarch was slackening.

The Queen was successful in raising money and plate for the war, and the people were enthusiastically on her side; moreover certain members of Olivares's own family were now turning against him because he had legitimized Enrique Felipe, and thus their chances of profit from their influential relative were lessened.

Philip's army was defeated by Marshall de la Motte before Lerida in 1642, and Philip was told that unless he changed his counsels he would lose his crown. When Philip returned to Madrid the Queen took their son, Baltasar Carlos, to him and implored him to cast off Olivares, if not for his own sake for that of the child. His old foster-mother, Ana de Guevara, waylaid him as he left the Queen and implored him to rid himself of Olivares. She reminded the King that Olivares had banished her and that she had only been able to return to the Court during his absence, for the sad fact was that Olivares wished to banish from the King's side all whom he loved, because he feared they might impair his own influence. The King was deeply moved by this and wrote to Olivares, telling him that he gave him leave to retire. Olivares could not believe that he was dismissed, but he was to discover that at last his enemies had separated him from the King. Philip went to the Escorial for two or three days so that he might not see the departure of the man who had been his intimate friend and counsellor for twenty-two years.

It has been suggested that the secret methods of the Inquisition were used to bring about Olivares's downfall, and that even when the ex-minister was living in obscurity there were those who sought to put an end to his life. As for Philip, he was a man of some sentiment, and he often thought of recalling Olivares; this would have aroused revolt, Philip knew, for he was constantly being urged that death should have been the reward of his ex-minister.

The people were demanding his head, and the Inquisition

would not have forgotten that he had once tried to destroy it; it may have been that it considered it could never allow such a man to continue to live.

The King must have come very near to granting the requests for vengeance on Olivares, for when the latter wrote to him asking to be allowed to end his exile, Philip answered that he must reign and his son must be crowned King of Aragon; yet he was afraid that this might not be unless he delivered the head of Olivares to the people.

This letter unnerved Olivares, and it is reported that on receiving it he went mad and died. This event took place on 22nd July, 1645, over two years after his dismissal.

## CHAPTER FIFTEEN

# THE INQUISITION UNDER PHILIP IV

All this time the Inquisition had been working as zealously as ever, the mental climate of the country suiting its unhealthy growth. The King, that conscience-stricken sensualist, was typical of his country's mood; and it was as though he believed that the poverty of the people and the disastrous relations with other countries could be hidden by this flaunting show of piety, these lavish ceremonies which were conducted with such pomp in the streets and had their hideous climax in the *quemadero*.

After the dismissal of Olivares the King desperately tried to reform his ways. He was beginning to believe that his conduct had brought his country's fortunes to this present state and he grew maudlin in his repentance.

It was at this time that he met Sor Maria de Agreda. He was travelling with Don Luis de Haro (the nephew of Olivares whom since the fall of the latter he had made one of his chief ministers, for Don Luis had turned against his uncle when he had brought forward Enrique Felipe and had him legitimized, when they visited the Convent of the Immaculate Conception at Agreda.

Sor Maria was the abbess; a woman of about forty at this time, she had written many mystical books and the King was eager to meet her; when he did so he was so impressed by her wisdom that he and she became lifelong friends.

He wrote to her regularly, consulting her on all matters. One letter of his begins by pointing out that he has left a wide margin so that she can comment on his remarks, and he tells her that the contents of the letter are for her eyes alone.

Six hundred letters passed between Sor Maria and the King during the twenty-two years of this strange friendship; she was Philip's chief adviser until she died in 1655; Philip himself died four months later.

Sor Maria was noted for her piety and the revelations which were reputed to have come to her; she was said to be in constant communication with God, the Virgin, and the angels.

When the Cortes of Aragon made complaints to Philip concerning the Inquisition, which was hated in Aragon to a greater extent than in Castile (for in Aragon the Inquisition was at its most powerful), Philip was perplexed. As one minister had said, the Inquisition was to Philip as one of his eyes; he felt that while he upheld it and it provided him with spectacular *autos de fé* he could feel that he had upheld the Faith of Spain and that if misfortune had come to him it must be through the will of God. Yet he feared a rising in Aragon which would cost him his crown.

On this occasion he did not ask the advice of his ministers but of the nun, Sor Maria. In spite of her mysticism she must have had a shrewd mind, and there is no doubt that she had a deep affection for the King. When he told her that he must preserve the Faith of Spain at all costs and therefore would support the Inquisition with all his might, she begged him to think again and consider what revolt in Aragon would mean at this stage of the country's fortunes. Catalonia was in revolt; what if the Aragonese joined the Catalonians? What would happen then to the unity of Spain?

As a result the officials of the Aragonese Inquisition lost many of their privileges; and this was apparent when the murder of Inquisitor Lazaeta occurred.

Inquisitor Lazaeta was having a love affair with a married woman in San Anton. The woman's husband, Miguel Choved, discovering this, prepared to trap the lovers, and told his wife that he was going on a journey. Choved's wife arranged that her lover should visit her after dark, which he did; the Inquisitor's coach was left in a near-by street and he went to the house to which some time later Choved came back. Lazaeta's coachman grew restive when his master did not return, and going in search of him found his dead body lying on the cobbles of a near-by alley. Both the Choveds disappeared, but a servant, Francisco Arnal, was arrested by the Inquisition for having helped to commit the murder.

The court of Justicia, however, intervened and there was

trouble between the ecclesiastical and secular courts. The Supreme Council then declared that it would be better to remove the Tribunal from Aragon than that it should be submitted to such humiliation. This was a clear indication of how the new laws had reduced the power of the Inquisition in Aragon.

In 1644 the Queen was suffering from erysipelas and some form of choleraic attack. She died in October. Only two children survived her – the heir, Baltasar Carlos, and Maria Teresa. The King was filled with grief, for in spite of his infidelities he had had a great affection for his pleasure-loving Queen whose character had not been unlike his own. Letters to Sor Maria continued to be written, when he implored her to intercede for him with the saints that he might overcome his misfortunes. Philip mourned for the poverty he saw in his country and wept for the misery of his people; yet at the same time he did little to curb his own extravagance. It was comforting to believe that everything that happened was due to the will of God; yet at the same time his conscience worried him; but that was soothed by the signs of piety in the punishment meted out to heretics in the great *autos de fé*.

Sor Maria wrote that he must purge Madrid of its sin. She heard that men and women promenaded in the Liars' Walk, and that their dress, conversation, and manners were far from becoming, and most unsuitable for subjects of this Catholic country.

Philip, becoming more and more under the spell of this nun, tried to carry out her advice and, much to the people's dismay and astonishment (for Philip had been a devotee of them), the theatres were closed. It is only fair to say that Sor Maria advised Philip to look closely into the system of the press-gang which, in seizing men to fight, caused great hardship to their families; and that her counsel was often followed to the good of the country.

In 1646 Baltasar Carlos began to suffer from tertian fever, and Philip was overcome with fear at this threat to the life of his heir. He wrote to Sor Maria that if he did not believe that his troubles were sent as warnings from Heaven, in order that he might prepare for the salvation of his soul, he could not endure them.

Baltasar Carlos was betrothed to Mariana of Austria, but later that year he succumbed to the fevers, and Philip's grief at the death of his beloved son was great. He became listless and left the governing of the country to his favourites, which distressed Sor Maria who told him she had had a vision of Baltasar Carlos who informed her that he was grieved to see his father surrounded by men who sought their own advantage rather than that of the nation. (At the time of the Queen's death Sor Maria had said she had had a vision of the Queen who had expressed her distress at the manners of the women of Madrid).

Philip answered her with more spirit than usual, pointing out that it was necessary for a king to employ ministers. He did not shirk his duty, he insisted, for he was constantly at his desk, his pen in his hand.

Sor Maria replied by urging him to take up arms once more against the French who had been defeated at Lerida.

The death of Baltasar Carlos had aroused anxieties concerning the succession, and the King, who was only forty-two, was urged by his ministers to marry again. They eyed the ambitious Don John of Austria with some misgiving, for he would not readily be accepted as king. Philip had one legitimate child – a daughter aged eight, Maria Teresa, who was eventually to marry Louis XIV. In 1649 Philip married his niece Mariana (the daughter of his sister, Maria). She was fifteen at the time of the marriage, and for a time Philip was absorbed in this union. He had been writing to Sor Maria explaining how hard he had tried not to indulge in amorous intrigues, and how the habit of a lifetime had been too much for him. Now he declared he would reform; he would never stray from the virtuous life; he would devote himself to his young wife, and he prayed that before long the union would be blessed with an heir – which was after all, the sole reason for its having taken place.

Philip soon tired of this child-wife and resumed the old habits, but in 1651 a daughter was born. This was Margaret Maria (whose portrait is to be seen in Velasquez's *The Maids of Honour*. To Philip Mariana was a child more suited to be the companion of his daughter, Maria Teresa, and he often referred to her as 'my niece' as though he had forgotten that she was also his wife and the Queen of Spain. Mariana grew homesick when she realized that the King had lost interest in her, and then she must have found the etiquette of the Spanish Court stifling. An example of Spanish formality is given by the conduct of young Maria Teresa at the christening ceremonies of Margaret Maria. Taking off her gloves, Maria Teresa dropped a very valuable diamond bracelet, but when a woman, in the crowd pressing about her, picked it up and handed it to her, she refused it, for it was a matter of etiquette that no royal person must take anything direct from a commoner. Hastily officials signed to the woman that she might keep the bracelet, so there was one person on that occasion who must have been very thankful for the formality of Spanish court manners. (Hume from Florez's *Reinas Catolicas*.)

Mariana bore other girls who died soon after their birth, and Philip – and the country – despaired of a male heir, but eventually in 1657, a boy was born, and named Philip Prosper.

Three years later Philip's daughter Maria Teresa, was married to Philip's nephew, *le Roi Soleil* (one of the results of a peace between the two countries); but Philip was still beset by anxieties, for the heir was proving to be a sickly little fellow and there was little hope of his reaching manhood. He died in November 1661; and Philip wrote to Sor Maria that he saw he had offended God and was being punished for his sins.

His health declined. He suffered, among other things, from gallstones, and when Sor Maria begged him to take care of his health he answered that he asked nothing but that God's will be done. Now that he felt himself to be growing near to his end his conscience was even more active; and because he was not blindly foolish he realized that his indolence and love of pleasure had had an adverse effect on the fortunes of Spain.

Ambitious Louis XIV was a dangerous neighbour; Mariana was already thinking of the time after Philip's death when she would be a power in the land. She had borne him another son, a very delicate boy, whose jaw was malformed so that he could not speak clearly, and who was obviously mentally deficient. But he was the heir to the throne and, while he lived and his mother could occupy the regency, her position would be a powerful one. Thus was the dying Philip aware of the desire for power which had been stirred within his niece-wife. Sor Maria had recently died and he was without her guidance.

In June 1665 the Spanish suffered great defeat at the hands

of the Portuguese who had been helped by the English since the marriage of Charles II of England to Catherine of Braganza; men and equipment had been lost and Philip had no means of providing more.

Dying Philip looked back over his life and saw to what a pass his great Empire had been reduced since the great days of Emperor Charles and Philip II – great-grandfather and grandfather. He believed that this was God's revenge for all those nights of revelling and illegitimate children, the number of whom he was uncertain.

He fell into such a mood of melancholy that many believed he was bewitched. There was a rumour that the Inquisitor-General had been trying to free the King from the spell, and that the evil forces had brought about his death for this reason. Many of the writers and artists at the Court laughed at these ideas and insisted that the ailments of the body had produced these symptoms; but the men of the Church insisted that Satan was responsible for the King's maladies, and the new Inquisitor-General, with the help of his confessor, went through the King's collection of relics, because they feared some evil charm might have been put among them.

In the Dominican monastery of the Atocha a book on witchcraft and some pictures of the King, in which pins had been stuck, were burned with solemnity.

Neither these remedies nor those of the physicians were effective, and on the 17th of September, 1665, Philip IV died.

It was during this reign that the Inquisition reached those heights of power which it was never to touch again; and the reason for this is seen in the character of the King which was reflected in the nature of the Court, which in its turn had its effect upon the mood of the people.

The King was weak but he longed to be good; and he saw in strict adherence to what he thought of as religious duty, the neutralizer of pleasure. He indulged in his debauches, but he supported the Inquisition; he committed his sins but he could confess and be given his penance, and all was well.

Thus the Inquisition was as his 'right eye' to him; his weak indecisive policy, his reliance on favourites, had brought low the temporal power of his country; but he had determined that that quality on which Philip II had insisted (the unity of faith) should be kept intact.

There was one quality in this King, though, the importance of which had not been seen during his reign. He had made of Madrid a great artistic centre, surrounding himself with writers and painters. He had found one of his greatest pleasures in the work of Velasquez in whose studio he had passed many pleasant hours. Thus he had brought into the country an element which was to make itself felt.

A new age of enlightenment was coming to Spain; and in that atmosphere the Inquisition would find its way made less easy; it would have to fight for its survival.

## CHAPTER SIXTEEN

# THE CASE OF VILLANUEVA

Throughout the history of the Inquisition there are many instances of trouble between the sovereigns of countries and the Papacy, the Pope being eager to retain control of ecclesiastical trials, the sovereigns determined that they should reign supreme in their lands. One of the most interesting and important examples which occurred during the reign of Philip IV is that of Gerónimo de Villanueva.

Gerónimo de Villanueva was Marquis of Villalba, an ancient Aragonese family. Olivares had favoured him – and consequently so had Philip – and he held many offices under the Crown.

Villanueva had been involved in the case of Teresa de Silva and the nuns of San Placido. It will be remembered that many of the nuns in the convent, including Teresa, their abbess, were reputed to be possessed by demons and indulged in the wildest conduct. Villanueva with the family of Teresa de Silva had supplied the money to found the convent of La Encarnacion Bedita de San Placido and had appointed Fray Francisco Garcia de Calderon as confessor. Calderon was denounced to the Inquisition in time and tried at Toledo, while the nuns were arrested and made to confess what the Inquisitors wished them to, with the result that Calderon was judged to be guilty of teaching heresy and of being an *alumbrado*. He was sentenced to perpetual imprisonment, Teresa was sent to a convent for four years, and the nuns placed in different convents.

Villanueva could not remain aloof from the scandals which had touched San Placido and Calderon. The house in which he lived adjoined the convent and he had spent a great deal of time there. During Calderon's trial it had leaked out that witnesses had actually seen him, his head on Teresa's lap, in most affectionate manner, while she hunted for lice in his head.

It was recalled that the revelations of Teresa and her nuns had concerned the future glory of the convent, Calderon and Villanueva. They had prophesied that Calderon would become Pope, reign for thirty-three years, and reform the world with the help of Villanueva.

The Inquisition decided that he was either guilty of practising heresy or of condoning it, but since Villanueva was a favourite of Olivares, who at that time ruled the King, the Inquisition was wary of bringing an accusation against him.

Yet Villanueva was fully aware of the power of the Holy Office and although Olivares and the King might wish to protect him, he knew that the latter was fanatically behind the Inquisition; so Villanueva presented himself to one of the chief Inquisitors, Antonio de Sotomayor, who later that year was to become Inquisitor-General, admitting that he had put his confidence mistakenly in Calderon, and that if he had sinned against the Church in doing so he was prepared to do penance.

While Villanueva was eager not to offend the Inquisition because of the King's regard for the institution, the Inquisition was eager not to offend *him* because of his standing with the King and Olivares, and he was proclaimed not guilty and a certificate was given to him accordingly.

Having secured his own acquittal he decided to work on behalf of the nuns that they might return to the convent. This would be a difficult matter, for if he could prove the nuns innocent that was tantamount to proving the Inquisition guilty of false judgment. However, Villanueva was shrewd and clever and although it took some time to make a case for the nuns he did this. They were, he insisted, innocent; they had done nothing but obey Calderon who had been set above them as their spiritual adviser. Was it wrong to obey a spiritual adviser? Nine judges were appointed to try the case again. Pressure from Villanueva, and possibly Olivares, made the nine judges eager to give the desired verdict; but they were again anxious not to offend the Inquisition. Their verdict was that the nuns were innocent, but the judges added that had they been asked to consider the evidence which had been laid before that tribunal they also would have pronounced them guilty.

Words were carefully chosen, gestures were very graceful;

the fact remained that Calderon became the scapegoat and the nuns returned to San Placido.

But the Inquisition had a long memory and it was scarcely likely that it felt very pleased with Villanueva. He had come safely out of the case of the possessed nuns because he had influential friends at Court, but once those friends were removed, it would not be necessary to treat him with such leniency. The storm was growing about Olivares and, if that minister fell from grace, the Inquisition need not have the same fear of reopening the case against Villanueva, for they often reopened cases when it was expedient to do so.

St Pius V had laid down the rule that acquittals for heresy should not be held *res judicata* and permanent, whoever pronounced them. The moment might not be propitious, but the Inquisition would continue to remain alert. Villanueva was a rich man and therefore a worthy prey; he had won a case against the Inquisition when he had re-established his nuns; it may have been that the Inquisition had its eyes on an even greater prize – Olivares, for there is an opinion that the Inquisition was behind the downfall of Philip's favourite minister. If Villanueva fell into the hands of the Inquisition, it would certainly be easy to discover evidence against Olivares. Therefore the Inquisition was waiting to bring Villanueva into its web.

There is a story of a scandal in which Villanueva, the King, and the nuns of San Placido were concerned.

As has been said, Villanueva's house was next door to the convent in the Calle de Madera, and he was a frequent visitor to the convent. He had also, with Olivares, helped to arrange the King's love affairs; and after the rehabilitation of the nuns he discovered one of them to be an exceptionally beautiful young woman, and told the King about her.

Philip, ever amorous, was captivated by the prospect of seducing a beautiful nun, and Villanueva, who had done so much for the convent with his money and influence, was able to take the disguised King inside the convent walls.

The nun however had taken her vows and the King could only speak to her through the grille, she declaring that they could not meet in any other way. The King grew impatient, and

Olivares and Villanueva, always ready to appease his desires, no doubt to keep him from meddling too much in state affairs, determined that his passion for the beautiful nun should be consummated.

Villanueva begged the nun to renounce her vows, and so that no time should be wasted, Philip growing more impatient as though for fear his conscience would begin to trouble him before the affair was completed, Villanueva set workmen making a passage from his cellars to the convent, so that, once the nun was ready, the King could visit her with the greatest ease whenever he wished.

The nun, however, in a moment of panic confessed to the abbess, Teresa, what was about to happen, and Teresa begged Villanueva to reconsider what he was doing and what would happen to him and the convent if it were discovered. Villanueva merely laughed at her. This adventure concerned the King; none, not even the Inquisition, would dare criticize what he did.

The passage was ready, the plans were made, and the nun was to be waiting for the King in that cloister which was now connected by the passage with the house next door.

The King, led by Villanueva, arrived in the cloister, to find it in gloom, except at that spot where tapers lighted a bier. Stretched out on this bier was the beautiful nun, in her hands a crucifix.

This dramatic gesture was typical of the hysterical Teresa, who had sought to deter the King presumably by the implication that the nun would better be dead than become his mistress.

Philip, whose superstitious fears were never far away and whose conscience was always stalking him, so we are are told, shivered at the sight of the woman on the bier and made with all speed through the secret passage to Villanueva's house.

According to the story, however, his desire was stronger than either superstition or conscience, and later the affair continued in less dramatic but more comfortable circumstances.

The affairs of kings have always been of great interest to their subjects, and it was not long before it was known that the King had a new mistress; and the Inquisition discovered that she was one of the nuns of San Placido – that convent which had been re-established after the tribunal had ordered that it should be disbanded and its inmates scattered.

It was a delicate matter since the King himself was so vitally concerned, but the Inquisitor-General, Sotomayor, who was Philip's confessor (and it had been thought by the King and Olivares, completely in the latter's power) was obliged to remonstrate with the King on his behaviour and to try to appeal to his conscience that he might stop visiting the nun; in which case it might be possible to bring a charge against Villanueva.

Olivares by this time was deeply conscious of powerful enemies all about him, and he felt the Inquisitor-General to be one of them, since he had dared remonstrate with the King.

An opportunity came to rid themselves of Sotomayor, and Olivares and the King took it. Although Philip usually gave his full support to the Inquisition he had on occasions stood out against it. Aragon had asked that all officials of the tribunals should be men of Aragon, and Philip had promised that he would use his influence with the Inquisition that this should be so. As a consequence he made several appointments which did not meet with the approval of the Inquisition and there was a certain controversy. The result of this was that, when a high position in the Tribunal was to be filled, a list of three names must be submitted to Philip that he might select from them; thus both King and Inquisition would, in a way, have a say in the selection. The Supreme Council had agreed to this but Sotomayor was not entirely satisfied.

For this reason (officially at least) he was made an offer. He must resign his position as Inquisitor-General and leave for Cordova when he would be given 12,000 ducats a year; if he failed to do this he would be dismissed from his office and banished from Spain. He might make his choice. It is obvious what Sotomayor's choice was.

When the Pope expressed his desire to examine the case of Villanueva, the Inquisition prepared to forward all the documents concerning him to Rome, and selected as their messenger a certain Paredes.

Olivares and the King determined that these papers should never fall into the Pope's hands if they could help it; they prevented Paredes leaving immediately and one of the Court painters did several sketches of him; these were hastily despatched to Philip's agents in the coast towns of Italy through which Paredes would have to pass on his way to Rome. With the sketches went orders that Paredes was to be kidnapped immediately he was sighted in Italy.

The plan succeeded, and no sooner had the messenger landed at Genoa than he was seized and imprisoned in the castle of Ovo at Naples. Poor man, because he had been selected as the Inquisition's messenger he was to spend the rest of his life – fifteen years – in prison there.

The papers he had been carrying with him were taken back to Olivares who, as soon as they were in his hands, took them to the King; they were destroyed in Philip's private apartment.

Sotomayor was followed as Inquisitor-General by Diego de Arce y Reynoso, Bishop of Plasencia, who wrote to the Pope asking his views on the case, but as the messenger and the documents had vanished there was no proof against Villanueva.

The disgrace of Olivares followed shortly and, with this favourite out of the way, Villanueva was no longer so secure. The Inquisition had a long memory and was determined to take him in the end.

Philip was in a state of melancholy; the affair with the nun had long petered out, and the King had no doubt overcome the worrying of his conscience concerning this and was probably engaged in another. Spain was in a desperate plight; three disastrous wars had imperilled her status, and now Philip had been deprived of the minister whom he had trusted to govern the kingdom for the last twenty years. The Inquisition felt that this was the moment to strike at Villanueva and it began with the Convent of San Placido.

A letter was drawn up to be signed by Philip, in which it was stated that the King was greatly concerned about the affair of the possessed nuns which had never been satisfactorily cleared up. Philip's signature on this was obtained without any difficulty and, as a result, Inquisitors visited the convent for the purpose of building up a new case against Villanueva.

There were fresh papers which indicated that Villanueva had been accustomed to writing down the words of the demons which came from the mouths of the nuns, that he had fervently believed in the existence of the demons, and dabbled in astrology. This was heresy against the Church, and the Inquisition felt itself justified in acting.

They chose their time carefully and waited until the King was away on the campaign in Catalonia.

At two o'clock in the afternoon at siesta time, two Inquisitors, Ortiz and Calaya, called on Villanueva, took him out to a coach, which was waiting, forced him inside and were quickly driven with him through the quiet streets out to Toledo.

Villanueva was put in a cell in which was a little cot; there he was kept in solitude, and Philip at that time could have had no notion of what had happened, for secret despatches continued to arrive for Villanueva which had to be dealt with by others; but when Philip was informed of the arrest and was told that it had been carried out in the service of the Faith, so subservient was he to the Inquisition, so eager to placate his God with his piety, that he did nothing to save Villanueva, declaring that he only lived to preserve the Holy Catholic Faith in his country.

The arrest caused apprehension in many quarters. The country was in danger and the Inquisition had arrested one of its principal ministers. Villanueva had been a very influential man and, if he had enemies, he also had friends. The kingdom of Aragon expressed its disapproval of the Inquisition's action, and it was said that a man of such a great family, which had for years served the state well, should have been treated with more dignity and imprisoned in a private house, if it was necessary to imprison him at all.

Philip, however, conscience-stricken by the weight of his peccadilloes – no doubt thinking of the nun on the bier – remained silent to the pleas, and gave his support to the Inquisition.

Villanueva, suffering from acute mental strain, became very ill and was allowed to have one of his servants to look after him; but when Philip returned to Madrid on account of the Queen's illness, he did nothing to help his old favourite.

Villanueva's trial lingered on according to the usual custom, and it was not until two years after his arrest that he was tried and sentenced.

He was found to be suspected of heresy, though not vehemently, and in February 1647 he was called to an audience chamber to hear his sentence. He was reprimanded for his conduct and warned that it must never occur again; he was to have nothing more to do with the nuns of San Placido and was never again to live in the house next door to the convent, but was to be banished for three years from Madrid and Toledo and twenty leagues around them.

Considering the fate of so many, this seems a light sentence; but it must be remembered that Villanueva had been one of the most important ministers in the country, and his career was ruined; he had suffered more than three years' imprisonment, and his family who were disgraced with him worked indefatigably to secure a remission of the sentence. His two brothers and one sister were all in important positions in the country (Ana had become abbess of San Placido, and one brother was a proctor, the other a Justíca). The Inquisition, however, was deaf to these appeals.

When Villanueva heard his sentence he was enraged, and in a frenzy of anger he shouted accusations at his judges; as a result he was taken back to his cell and later put in a secret prison where he was treated with much harshness.

He had been commanded to abjure *de levi* and this he refused to do until he was warned that failure to comply meant that he would be handed to the secular arm to be condemned to the stake.

Agustin, the Justíca, worked hard for his brother and applied to Rome; Philip also appealed to the Pope pointing out that if he used his influence on Villanueva's behalf after the Inquisition had sentenced him, this would be harmful to the Catholic Faith; but Joseph Navarro, who had been sent to Rome by Agustin, was able, in spite of the protests of Philip's ambassador, to obtain Papal permission for an appeal.

Villanueva, hearing what was happening and realizing that the Pope was far away and he was as the mercy of Philip and the Inquisition, wrote to Philip telling him that although Papal permission had been granted for an appeal against his sentence he was ready to forgo this if it was the will of the King. The Inquisitor-General meanwhile refused to accept the Papal brief. This was one of the most notorious differences between the Papacy and the Inquisition in Spain.

The King and the Inquisitor-General were ready to plunge into conflict with the Pope – Innocent X – but a junta of six of the leading statesmen of Spain summed up their views of the case; and even those who were not on the side of Villanueva decided that, in view of the present ferment in Naples which might lead to revolt, it would be very unwise to arouse the Pope's anger against Spain, for then Spanish possessions in Italy might be in real danger.

Had it not been for the views of this junta, Villanueva would undoubtedly have been persecuted further.

Innocent was furious at the manner in which his brief had been treated, and threatened Arce, the Inquisitor-General, with excommunication and dismissal from his post. Arce wrote placatingly to Innocent telling him that Villanueva had been treated with justice and even kindness and that it was necessary for the Inquisition to have great power, for heresy was spreading throughout the country in an alarming fashion. He asked that the Pope should allow the Supreme Council to deal with the case.

Innocent however was determined to obtain obedience and appointed bishops to try the case. None was very eager for the task, fearing the power of the Inquisition, but at last the Bishop of Avila accepted. However Villanueva, growing more and more fearful of the storm which his case was arousing, did not appear before Avila to have the case reconsidered. But the Pope was not prepared to let the matter drop. This was more than the case of one man justly or unjustly accused by the Inquisition; it was a recurrence of the old fight. The Pope was demanding supremacy for the Papacy, while the Spanish Inquisition and the King of Spain were seeking independence of Rome.

The wrangle continued, and letters went back and forth between Madrid and Rome, both sides manoeuvring for position, and Villanueva, the cause of it all, wishing to escape and live in peace. Inquisitor-General Arce was fervently advising the King to resist the Pope, knowing that if he did not he himself would be the one to suffer, while Philip's statesmen were urging caution. Preparations for war with Italy were begun, and all ships from Italy coming into Spanish ports were subjected to close scrutiny, for Philip had forgotten that he did not possess the strength of Emperor Charles and Philip II which would have enabled him to defy the Pope.

Innocent threatened to abolish the Spanish Inquisition; Arce retorted that God would never allow it. But Philip by this time was beginning to understand his danger. Arce, seeing this and thinking only of his own, implored Philip for the sake of the Holy Catholic Faith, not to yield. But Philip decided to take the advice of the junta.

Innocent then suggested that Arce should retire to his See of Plasencia, since it was many years since he had been there; this was tantamount to commanding him to resign his position of Inquisitor-General, and Arce was both incensed and terrified. His reply was to relinquish the bishopric of Plasencia.

But the Pope was winning the battle. Philip could see that he had no alternative but to send to Rome what documents remained concerning Villanueva's case, and doing so, begged the Pope not to open the case, for if he did so he was humiliating not only the King but the Spanish Inquisition.

Innocent was however not so much interested in the case of Villanueva as in establishing his supremacy over Spain. He had no wish to consider the matter and announced his intention of passing it over to certain bishops.

The affair dragged on inconclusively because the fate of Villanueva was important to neither side, and in July 1653 Villanueva died.

The wrangle between the Papacy and Spain continued even after Villanueva's death into the reign of Alexander VII.

## CHAPTER SEVENTEEN

# CHARLES THE BEWITCHED

When Philip's near-imbecile son, Charles II, came to the throne it appeared that everything of Spain was on the decline except the Inquisition. To all outward appearances that remained as powerful as ever, and in 1680, fifteen years after the death of Philip IV, one of the greatest *autos de fé* ever seen was celebrated in the Plaza Mayor of Madrid. Charles and his Queen honoured the occasion with their presence and 105 people were brought out of their prisons to receive their sentences. Outside the gate of Fuencarral, the *quemadero* of the occasion, the bonfire was 60 feet square and 7 feet high.

So the Inquisition was in its full glory while the country was in a desperate state. The expulsion of Jews and Moors had depopulated Spain to an extent which was alarming; excessive taxation had impoverished the people; and foreigners were snatching the trade which had once been Spain's.

The King had been a poor creature from birth and could not provide the country with an heir. He had been four years old when his father died, and his mother, whom Philip had appointed to be Regent during his son's minority, had proved herself to be a woman determined on acquiring power.

Mariana was an Austrian and her aim was to strengthen alliances with her own kinsmen and the friendship with France which was being made possible by the marriage of Maria Teresa and Louis XIV.

Although Mariana had declared, when she took over the Regency, that she would not allow favourites to govern the kingdom, she had soon arranged special favours for her confessor, Father Juan Everardo Nithard; and before long he was not only given a place on the Regency Council but was made Inquisitor-General.

Trouble was inevitable considering the circumstances: a

child-king, a Regent who was a foreigner and favoured foreigners such as Nithard, a country weak from the effects of taxation and wars, and a handsome young hero in Philip's illegitimate son by the actress, Maria Calderon – Don John of Austria.

Like his famous namesake he could not entirely avert his eyes from the crown; he sought to control the government and it was not long before he was taking sides against the Queen and her favourite Nithard.

Don John had a real grievance against the Queen and Nithard when Malladas, one of his intimate friends, was arrested by the Queen's orders for no apparent reason, except that he was a friend of Don John and therefore presumed to be an enemy. Malladas was strangled in prison a few hours after his arrest, having had no trial and not even knowing the reason for his arrest.

Don John could not be expected to accept such conduct without protest, and when he made known his disapproval he was told to leave Court.

More of his friends were arrested and rumours of plots against the Queen were circulated. An order for Don John's arrest was issued, but he did not wait for it to be carried out; he escaped to Barcelona and was there received with acclaim.

Now the country was ready to take sides and – as Don John was young, handsome and something of a hero, and Nithard was German – the late King's illegitimate son found himself at the head of the more popular party.

The Queen tried to placate her late husband's son, but Don John stated that the only way to a reconciliation was for her to dismiss Nithard; and with the army which had gathered about him he marched to Madrid.

The country was behind Don John in his demand, and the Queen saw that the only way in which she could save herself was to dismiss her favourite.

Nithard went to Rome where he stayed until his death in 1681 and, as the country was then more sympathetic towards the Queen, Don John realized that he should not go too far. There was a compromise, and Don John was made Viceroy of Aragon.

In spite of her declaration that the reign of favourites was over in Spain, no sooner had Nithard disappeared into exile than Mariana began showering honours on Valenzuela. Here was a man of great ambition, determined to rule the country and its Queen Regent. Young Charles did not count, of course; he was too delicate to have received a proper education, and up to the age of ten had been treated as though he were a baby. He was completely under the domination of his mother whom it suited that he should remain powerless to govern.

The energetic Valenzuela proved himself so useful to the Queen that he was not only managing affairs of state but had also found a place for himself in her bed. Mariana's grateful appreciation was apparent in the titles she bestowed on him, and he was fast becoming the most powerful man in Spain, so that all those who wished for advancement knew they must please him.

Such a man must inevitably arouse enmity, and there was Don John with his jealous eyes on the throne and on his young half-brother who was now fifteen, that age when, it had been ordained in the will of Philip IV, he should come of age.

Don John and his partisans tried to persuade Charles to sign an order commanding Don John to return to Madrid. Not only was Don John to be recalled but to be made first minister. But Valenzuela heard what was happening before this order was signed, and the Queen, who had always governed her son, was able to prevent his putting his signature to the order; so Don John's schemes for ruling through the King and thus displacing Valenzuela, who ruled through the Queen, failed; and it was Valenzuela who remained Prime Minister, taking up residence in the palace.

Meanwhile the condition of the people in Madrid was growing worse. Letters written at the time state that it was not uncommon to see people dying of starvation in the streets. In Philip II's time the population had been about 400,000; it was at this time about 200,000; and Madrid was typical of other towns. The starvation of the people was due to loss of that agricultural land which it had been the Moors' special talent to cultivate. Trade, which had flourished largely on account of the Jewish population, had been taken by other countries.

Countries in trouble look for a scapegoat, and Valenzuela

was chosen by the people on this occasion. Charles was induced to escape from the influence of his mother and her lover, and in January 1677 he left the palace and from a distance, with counsellors who were the enemies of Mariana and her lover, he ordered his mother to remain a prisoner there. Meanwhile Don John marched towards the capital, where he was received with joy. He gave his terms for undertaking the government of the country – which were that the Queen was to leave the capital for Toledo, and Valenzuela be arrested and banished from the country. These terms were agreed on and Valenzuela, after a short imprisonment, was sent to the Philippines and later went to Mexico where he remained until his death.

But Spain under Don John's dictatorship was no happier than it had been under that of the Queen Regent. Conceited, eager that all should remember his royal blood, Don John was more concerned in keeping the Queen Mother a prisoner than in righting the ills of Spain. He gave his time to the discussion of etiquette and whether or not French fashions should be adopted, while Louis XIV was conducting a successful campaign against Catalonia and waging war in Flanders. The people were asking themselves why they had revolted against the Queen Regent in favour of Don John, when under his rule the condition of the country had gone from bad to worse.

The peace of Nimeguen was signed in 1648 and a marriage was arranged between Charles and Princess Marie Louise of Orléans, the daughter of the French King's brother and Henrietta, sister of Charles II of England.

This was a direct blow at the Queen Mother who had hoped for a union between the King and a member of her own family. It is surprising that she should have wished for such a match, with the example of her son before her. Charles, with a tongue so large that his speech was unintelligible, and a chin so ill-shaped that his food had to consist mainly of slops because he could not chew, who had been carried about as a baby until he was ten years old, was the result of Hapsburg marrying Hapsburg. However, if Mariana realized this, it did not perturb her, for she was only concerned with the power she could bring to her Austrian family; but realizing that she could do nothing but accept the French marriage, she did this with as good a grace as possible; and the beautiful, rather giddy French princess, who had been brought up at the most glittering Court in Europe, came to Spain as the bride of a creature who was almost a degenerate.

It may have been that had Don John lived he would have been defeated by the Queen Mother's supporters. He died in September 1679. Fever and the ague were said to be the causes of death, but there were the usual rumours of poison; for, said the Queen Mother's enemies, she was determined to remove the man who had taken her place.

Charles was delighted with his gay bride; naturally she was less delighted, and there was great scandal when she insisted on introducing French manners to the Court. She snapped her fingers at Spanish solemnity, smiled, and even laughed in public; she insisted on behaving as she had at Versailles, introduced new comedies which were played at Court, ate and drank too freely and was ready to smile and converse with the common people.

The royal *ménage* must have been incongruous with its gay and carefree Queen and its King who was incapable of speaking intelligibly and who indulged in childish pleasures such as running wildly through the rooms of the palace from one balcony to another, quite purposelessly, as a very young child might.

Mariana was back in power, but she still had to contend with the maudlin devotion of Charles for his beautiful wife. As for Marie Louise, she had selected two favourites who scarcely ever left her and advised her in all things. These were Madame Quintin, a widow who had married an equerry in Marie Louise's French suite, and the equerry, Viremont himself. Those who wished to remove them from the Queen, tried to do so by bringing an accusation of immorality against them, but the Queen defended them so fiercely to the King that they were allowed to remain at Court.

An elaborate scheme was then devised for proving that they had tried to poison the King; and Charles, always terrified of poison, insisted that they be removed. Marie Louise's enemies whispered to the King that she had been involved in the plot, and thus brought about the end of her influence with Charles.

There was no child of this marriage, and in 1689, only ten

years after her arrival in Spain, Marie Louise died, believed by many to have been poisoned.

Before the year was out Charles was married to Mary Anne of Neuburg, daughter of the Elector Palatine. The new wife proved to be eager for power, and a party was formed of which she was the head and which had the support of the Queen Mother.

There were no children of this marriage and it was now obvious that Charles was impotent; therefore the succession to the Spanish throne was the subject of much speculation throughout Europe.

Wily Louis XIV was scheming to bring Spain under the influence of France. He was a grandson of Philip III and had married a daughter of Philip IV. Emperor Leopold was also a grandson of Philip III and had married a daughter of Philip IV. Both Louis and Leopold therefore kept alert eyes on Spain.

Mariana died in 1696 and Charles's health was failing lamentably. Terrified of being poisoned, he suspected his Queen of wishing him out of the way. He realized the difference between the flighty French princess who had been his first wife, and the scheming German who was his second; and he must have longed for the old days. Queen Mary Anne was determined that the succession should go to the son of the Emperor and was at great pains to keep from the King's side any who might influence him in favour of the French.

The battle continued over the dying King, who, although not yet forty, was suffering from senile decay; his wits were quite unable to cope with the intrigue, and the jostling for position continued.

The King's confessor, Father Matilla, had been procured for him by the Queen, and he influenced the King to such an extent that it seemed the German faction must be triumphant. But there was in the King's entourage a nobleman named Count Benavente, who became the secret tool of the French faction. One night Benavente secretly brought the Archbishop of Portocarrero to the King's private apartments, and to him Charles was induced to confess his fears of his wife. The Archbishop and Benavente then decided that the King must be rescued and that the first move would be to banish the confessor, Matilla, from the King's side, and appoint a new one, favourable to the French faction.

Matilla was replaced by Froilan Díaz, and within a few days Matilla had mysteriously died.

Froilan Díaz discovered that in the convent of Cangas some of the nuns were said to be possessed by demons, and he believed – a belief which was generally accepted – that during the ceremony of exorcism, when the demons were terrified of being banished from the bodies they were inhabiting, they could be forced to reveal facts which were outside the knowledge of ordinary people.

Díaz suggested that the demons in the nuns of Cangas might be made to tell the reason for the King's illness, for if the cause were known, the cure could more easily follow.

It had long been thought that the King had been bewitched and that was the reason for his ill-health. The Supreme Council of the Inquisition had even discussed taking steps to discover whether this was due to sorcery, but had done nothing.

In 1695 the Inquisitor-General, Valladares, had died and been succeeded by Juan Tomás de Rocaberti, Archbishop of Valencia; and the King in secret consulted Rocaberti, asking him to discover whether there was any truth in the theory that he had been bewitched.

Rocaberti put the King's request to the Suprema which still considered the matter highly dangerous. During the last reign the Inquisition had lost a little ground. Philip IV had been its devoted slave, but he had at the same time encouraged the writers at his Court, and ideas had begun to simmer in the minds of Spaniards. When complaints had been made concerning the Inquisition a commission had been set up to look into its activities, and this had been composed of fearless men who had boldly announced that the Inquisition, far from contributing to the good of the nation, was often a danger to it. In view of this the Inquisition was wary.

Froilan Díaz as King's confessor had a seat on the Suprema and he asked Rocaberti to help him discover whether Charles was bewitched. This Rocaberti promised to do, and he himself visited Cangas where he wrote the names of the King and

Queen on paper which he enclosed in his doublet. He then had one of the possessed nuns brought to him and demanded to know whether either of the people whose names were written on the paper in his doublet had been bewitched.

The 'demon' replied: Yes, one of the people had been bewitched. It was the King. When he was fourteen, on 3rd April, 1675, his mother had given him a cup of chocolate; in this cup was a spell made from certain parts of a dead man's body, and its object was to render the King impotent and so feeble in mind that he would be unable to govern the kingdom.

Could the King escape from the spell? was the next question. Yes, was the answer. He must be separated from his Queen, anointed with oil which had been blessed, and subjected to constant purging.

For a whole year the Inquisitor-General and Díaz tried to extract more information from the demons, but they – or the nuns – were mischievous. First they said he had not been bewitched at all, and they were only amusing themselves in saying that he had been. Then they said that he had been bewitched on a second occasion in 1694.

Poor Charles was anointed, purged and exorcized – all of which operations, far from improving his health, made it deteriorate.

Meanwhile another candidate for the Spanish throne had appeared in the field. This was the Electoral Prince of Bavaria, grandson of Empress Margaret, Philip IV's younger daughter, who had been the first wife of the Emperor Leopold.

Louis XIV was anxious, for it appeared that this last candidate might be the most favoured, and he slyly proposed that the Spanish crown should be divided among the three pretenders. This caused grave concern, as Louis knew it would: one of the greatest fears of all who cared for the good of Spain was to see it divided as it had been before the days of Ferdinand and Isabella. Oddly enough the Prince of Bavaria, who was only six years old, died mysteriously, so once more there were only two contestants in the field.

The Queen was fuming. Separated from her husband, her power was clipped, and she could see the French faction gaining all the ground that she had lost; and when she heard that the demons had said Charles had been bewitched a second time, in 1694, she was more than furious, she was alarmed, for this, she knew, was intended as a direct thrust against herself.

Four weeks after she had heard of this second bewitching Rocaberti died in suspicious circumstances, and the Queen did all in her power to have one of her men, Fray Antonio Folch de Cardona, appointed Inquisitor-General. But Charles was now highly suspicious of his Queen and determined to get to the bottom of his bewitchment. He therefore ignored the Queen's proposal and appointed Cardinal Alonso Fernandez de Cordova y Aguilar, who swore he would pursue the matter vigorously until he had sifted the truth and could lay it before the King.

Poor Aguilar! He had taken on a more dangerous task than he could have realized. He became ill and in a few days he was dead. His death coincided with the confirmation from Rome of his appointment.

By this time the King was growing very feeble and the Queen had regained some of her old power – enough for her to appoint the next Inquisitor-General, who was Balthasar de Mendoza y Sandoval. She had determined on the downfall of Díaz and those who had sought to involve her in this tale of demons and spells; Mendoza's reward was to be a cardinal's hat.

As a result an exorcizer, Fray Tenda, was arrested and during his examination he described what had happened at Cangas, involving Díaz, who was then questioned. Díaz answered that he had acted on instructions from Rocaberti at the request of the King, and that he could answer no question without the King's consent. Mendoza then asked for the King's consent to bring a charge against Díaz. The King's mind was now so bemused that it was easy for the Queen to persuade him to give his consent.

Díaz was ordered by Mendoza to go to the Dominican convent in Valladolid, and set out to do this, but before reaching Valladolid he decided that he would escape the Inquisition by seeking refuge in Rome. But Mendoza ordered his arrest, and he was brought back and put in the secret prison at Murcia.

Eventually Díaz was brought to Madrid and imprisoned in

the Dominican house of Nuestra Señora de Atocha. Here he remained for four four years, after which time he was found suspect of heresy.

His case developed into another of those long-drawn-out wrangles between the Pope and the Suprema, while the prisoner in his dungeon was disregarded.

However Díaz was reinstated in the Supreme Council after the death of Charles, and was rewarded with the See of Avila, for all that he had suffered; but the Pope, Clement XI, refused confirmation of the appointment because the Inquisition had failed to show him the papers concerning the case, and he was not sure of the justice of the acquittal. The new King, Philip V, would not allow anyone else to accept the See and it remained vacant until after the death of Díaz.

As Charles's death grew nearer the wrangling over the succession became more intense. The Pope came out on the side of the French, and Louis XIV intimated that if an attempt were made to put the Archduke on the throne he would oppose it with force.

Poor Charles, surrounded by holy relics, pestered on all sides, made a will in which he stated that his heir was to be Philip of Anjou.

The Queen immediately used her powers to persuade him to change his mind, with such persistence that Charles then said that the throne of Spain should go to the Archduke, but no alteration was made in the will.

Charles the Bewitched died in November 1700, aged thirty-nine, and it is said that he looked like a man of eighty. Thus ingloriously had lived and died the last Hapsburg king of Spain.

Philip of Anjou, to be Philip V of Spain, began the new dynasty; the Bourbons had arrived. Handsome, virile, seventeen years of age, he had the powerful King of France behind him. The French Ambassador was given a seat on the Council – a concession, insisted Louis XIV, which must be granted to all future ambassadors – the Austrian faction was banished from power, and the Queen retired to Toledo.

To welcome the new King of Spain an *auto de fé* was

arranged in his honour. To the astonishment of all, Philip declined the invitation to attend.

This was a sign of things to come. Spain would change under the rule of the Bourbons.

## CHAPTER EIGHTEEN

# THE INQUISITION AND THE BOURBONS

Philip's slight to the Inquisition did not mean that he objected to it on humanitarian grounds. He had been brought up in the reflection of *le Roi Soleil*, and therefore believed that there could be only one head of a state: its King. Philip made this clear from the beginning, and the Inquisition was immediately put into a different position from that which it had occupied during preceding reigns.

Philip was entirely French; Louis XIV had impressed on him before he left for Spain never to forget that he was a Frenchman, and in this at least he obeyed his grandfather. He was young and thoughtless and it was not long before the high places about the throne were filled by Frenchmen; French fashions were introduced and the name Austrian became a term of abuse to be hurled at any who criticized that which was French.

It was hardly likely, after there had been such controversy concerning Philip's claim to the throne, that he would be allowed to enjoy it in peace. The Emperor was furious; Queen Mary Anne, supported by the Inquisitor-General, let it be known that Charles II had changed his mind about his heir – on his deathbed – and had nominated the Archduke as future King of Spain. What Philip's accession meant to the bloated power of Louis XIV was at the root of much dissatisfaction. William III of England was furious with Louis for regarding James II as still King of England. Thus began the War of Succession which was to drag on until that year that Philip could truly call himself King of Spain.

He did win the applause of his people by placing himself at the head of his soldiers and himself leading them into battle – a kingly habit to remind the Spaniards of the Emperor Charles.

His bride was Marie Louise, the daughter of Victor

Amadeus of Savoy. She was only fourteen, and as soon as Philip saw her he fell in love with her and was to prove an uxorious husband.

As the girl was so young, Louis XIV, aided by Madame de Maintenon, sent with her as her counsellor a clever old woman, Anne Marie de la Trémouille, who was known in France as La Princesse des Ursins because she was the widow of Flavio Orsini, Duke of Bracciano. The task assigned to her by Louis and Madame de Maintenon was to establish her influence over the King and his bride, and obey the instructions which would reach her from Versailles. This the Princesse did very successfully. By Marie Louise, Philip had four children one of whom was that Luis in whose favour he abdicated, and another Ferdinand VI.

Philip fought with great gallantry which won him the respect of his people, but the War of Succession was long and there were many victories for the enemy. Philip had against him the genius of Marlborough who scored successes over the Spaniards in the Netherlands and distinguished himself at Blenheim, Ramillies, Oudenarde and Malplaquet; and when the league between Holland, Denmark, Austria, Prussia and England was formed he began to develop that melancholy hypochondria which was a feature of his later life and which was to dim all the bright hopes which the coming of a virile young man had raised in the hearts of so many Spaniards.

In 1714 Philip was at peace with the world apart of course from the Emperor, who would never accept him as King of Spain. Flanders had been lost in the struggle but Flanders had always been an uncertain blessing.

Marie Louise died that year and Philip was very unhappy. The Princesse des Ursins, however, continued to advise him, and during that time of mourning she was the only one whom he seemed to want near him. When he left the Court for the Palace of Medina Celi and the Princesse was lodged in a nearby monastery, in order that she might be at his instant call, the monks were asked to leave and a connecting passage was made between the monastery and the palace so that they could be in constant communication. So much did he rely on her that it was said he might marry her, even though she was old enough to have been his grandmother.

Instead he married Elizabeth Farnese, who was niece and stepdaughter of the Duke of Parma. The Princesse approved of this match. Elizabeth had been brought up simply, and she believed the girl would be easily subdued; such a marriage, the Princesse told Louis XIV, would enable Philip to regain his power in Italy.

The Princesse was soon to discover her mistake. Elizabeth may have been brought up simply, but she was ambitious and arrogant in the extreme. The truth was quickly disclosed to her for Elizabeth did not hurry to meet the King on her arrival in Spain, and delayed unnecessarily during the journey, in the Princesse's view. As soon as they met the Princesse delivered a mild reproach at which Elizabeth cried out imperiously that she would not be insulted by that old fool, who was to leave her presence at once.

Elizabeth made it clear that there was no room at her Court for the old Princess who was put in a coach an hour after their meeting, dressed as she was for the Court ceremony, not having been given time to change, and on a wintry night was driven out of Spain . . . a reward for thirteen years' devoted service to the King and his first wife!

Philip was very soon in the power of this new one who continued to rule him throughout his life. By Elizabeth he had six children and their mother schemed ambitiously, trying to jostle them into the highest positions.

By 1724, Philip became more melancholy than ever; he was convinced that he was ill, and was perpetually watching for new symptoms. His wife was his constant companion, advising him on all state matters; his days were spent in talking with her, in prayer and discussion of his ailments.

In January 1724 he announced to the world that he had become too infirm to rule, and that he was about to abdicate in favour of his eldest son Luis. He himself would retire to the Palace of St Ildefonsa de la Granja which he had built after the manner of Versailles, whence he could gaze towards France, and there he would live in obscurity with his wife to nurse him.

He wrote a letter to Luis in which he gave him his advice with such a religious fervour as might have belonged to Philip II. Luis was to maintain the Faith throughout the land. He was to give his support to the Inquisition, which had preserved

Catholicism in Spain and kept out heresy so that Spain was the most purely Catholic country in the world.

Philip had changed from the virile young man who had come to the throne nearly twenty-five years before. Overtaken by religious mania and melancholia he shut his eyes to the fact that industry in Spain had almost come to a standstill, partly because of the expulsion of Jews and Moors whose financial genius and industry would have saved it, partly because of the absurd *alcabalas* which imposed a tax so severe that Spanish manufacturers could not compete with those abroad. He could not have realized the growing power of England, which was almost entirely heretic and was on the way to building up an Empire which was to be even greater than the Spanish one had been in its prime. All over Europe new ideas were springing up, men were discussing reforms, not only in religion, but in economics. Such ideas were barred from Spanish territory and would continue to be so while the Inquisition held sway. Yet this state of affairs Philip, in his condition of religious melancholy, believed must persist – as long as the Inquisition realized that it was second to the monarchy.

Luis, who had been born in Spain, pleased the Spaniards; he was young, handsome and amiable, and soon earned the name of Luis the Well-beloved; but seven months after his accession he caught smallpox and died, and as the next son, Ferdinand, was only eleven, there was nothing for Philip to do but re-assume the crown.

Philip obviously did not fulfil the promise he had brought with him to Spain. Had he been a stronger man, less ready to be influenced by his wives, it is possible that the power of the Inquisition might have been decidedly crippled during his reign. He came from France, the most intellectual Court in Europe; his manners were French; his ideas were French; he had been well primed in his duties by Louis XIV – not that he always followed his grandfather's advice.

He believed that he, as King, should give encouragement to the arts, and that he should bring the men and women of his country in line, intellectually, with those across the Pyrenees. There must therefore be a literature; but a literature to be of any use must be a free literature, and how was it possible for such to survive in a country dominated by the Inquisition? He founded the National Library, the Academies of Languages, History, and Medicine, and the Seminary of the Nobles. But the censorship remained, and a great many of those ideas which were circulating in other parts of Europe were kept out of Spain.

Moreover Philip was not strong enough to bring any great change to Spain, as seen in the affair of Belando and Giudice.

He had broken off relationship with Rome because in 1709, during the War of Succession, Clement XI had recognized the Archduke Charles as King of Spain; and as a result Philip dismissed the nuncio and stopped money being sent to Rome. The old quarrel between Papacy and monarchy had broken out again, and in this the Inquisitor-General, Francesco Giudice, became involved. He was dismissed and banished.

Belando wrote a history of the times – giving a truthful account of this affair – which was to be dedicated to Philip and his Queen. The King and Queen read the history and accepted the dedication, but when that which Belando had written was brought to the notice of the Inquisition the book was seized by them on account of its exposure of the Giudice affair.

Belando was brought before the Tribunal and even when he offered to eliminate the offending passages, the offer was ignored and he was put into prison. Later he was sent to a convent where he was to spend the rest of his life, and was ordered to produce no more books.

This was in direct defiance of that freedom which was to produce a worthy literature, but the King allowed this to happen because by this time, 1744, he was too overcome by his religious mania to move in the matter.

This happened two years before his death. He had for some time believed he was near death, expressing even more abnormal interest in the minor ailments of his body than was habitual with him. His religious mania had grown to such an extent that their were periods towards the end of his life when he was considered to be insane; had he been a stronger man, had he not been so ready to be influenced by his wives and their favourites, he might have done a great deal more than he did for the country he ruled. His intentions had been of the best; his weak good nature, his absorption with his health and his superstitious fear of the afterlife had come between him and greatness.

On 9th July, 1746, Philip had an apoplectic fit and died. He had left the country a little better than he had found it. Although the Inquisition had worked incessantly during his reign and the brutalities had continued, a few new ideas had penetrated from a more enlightened country. The long and costly War of Succession, with which Philip's reign had begun, had more than anything else prevented his being the great ruler he might have been; his second wife's rabid ambition for her children had been another factor against him; but the weakness in his own character was more responsible than anything else. Yet with the coming of the first of the Bourbons, it seems that a little light was being shed on that tragic country; and in spite of the fact that the Inquisition still appeared to be a great power in the land, its foundations were beginning to tremble.

Although the Inquisition had been working as zealously as ever during the reign of the first Bourbon, perhaps on account of that sovereign's attitude the ceremonies had not been conducted with that fierce publicity which had been a feature of past *autos*. Hume in his *Spain; its Greatness and Decay* says that during the reign of Philip there were 782 *autos*, and that 14,000 people were sentenced. Edward Armstrong however, who revised Hume's history, says that Hume has taken his figures from Llorente, whom Edward Armstrong does not trust. Quoting Lea he says that there are authentic statistics only for the years between 1721 and 1727. During these years 77 people were burned in actuality and 74 in effigy; 811 were penanced; thus making the figures for the actual records 962 while those given by Llorente were 1785.

Whatever the figures, there is enough evidence to show that, during the reign of Philip, the Inquisition continued to work with accustomed zeal.

Ferdinand VI was of a kindly nature; this must have been the case because he was magnanimous towards his stepmother, Elizabeth Farnese, who had intrigued against him in the hope of securing the throne for her own son Charles. He was more eager than his father to bring culture to Spain and, like his father, he was ruled by his wife, Queen Barbara. They both wished to live a peaceful family life, free from the cares of state, and it was largely due to them that Spain remained aloof during the War of Independence when both France and England sought to draw her into the quarrel. Ferdinand was prudent, a true lover of peace, and under his rule prosperity began to return slowly to Spain, for during his reign the strength of the Spanish fleet increased considerably and there was no longer bankruptcy in the treasury.

Unfortunately in August 1758 Queen Barbara died, and the King's grief was so intense that he shut himself away in complete solitude, and there were periods when he lost his reason. He died in August 1759, exactly a year after Barbara's death.

The change, which his thirteen years of rule had brought about, was apparent. Scholars were now finding their way into Spain, visiting the academies which had been set up by the Bourbon kings; this inevitably brought about a new age of enlightenment and, most important of all, the position of the Inquisition was subtly changing, for people were looking askance at an institution which had brought terror into many lives over many generations. With the spread of culture, a certain amount of superstition was bound to disappear. As fewer people were brought before the tribunals there were no longer the large-scale confiscations; salaries of Inquisitors could not be increased and the cost of living had risen considerably. There was no longer the same desire to accept posts within the Inquisition. Thus it was necessary to employ people of lower standing who were less eager to do their work than their predecessors had been. Inevitably the great fear and respect in which the Inquisition had been held began to diminish.

Charles III, returning from Naples over which he had been ruling as King of the Two Sicilies, took the throne on the death of his half-brother Ferdinand; and in Charles III the Spaniards had the most intelligent of the Bourbons.

Charles was a patron of arts, even more determined than his father and brother to bring culture to Spain; he was equally determined to be ruler of the country and was less respectful to the Inquisition than any preceding monarch had ever been. Yet he did not seek to suppress the Inquisition, and is reputed to have given his reason as this: 'The Spaniards want to keep it and it gives me no trouble.' He had in fact made sure that it should give him no trouble, for in 1768 he had imposed new rules on censorship and later had taken from it the power to judge crimes other than heresy that it might not interfere with the secular courts. In that year 1768 it was decided that the King was the patron of the Inquisition and therefore possessed the *rights* of patronage. As patron the King should prevent violence and extortion.

But during the last years of Charles's reign the Inquisition discovered a new form of heresy, in the new ideas which, for all its vigilance, it could not prevent from seeping into the country from across the border.

Some of the King's most important ministers were suspected, but times had so changed that the Inquisitors had no power to arrest such men on suspicion. To do so they would need the King's consent and these men were too important to the King to be handed to the Inquisition merely because they held certain opinions.

Although they dared not touch men of influence they sought to make an example of men of lesser importance as in the case of Dr Luis Castelanos of Cadiz who was a philosopher and an agnostic. He was brought before the Tribunal and sentenced to confiscation and abjuration, to wear a *sanbenito* and to serve ten years in a hospital at Oran.

But the most important case of this time is that of Pablo Olavide, who had been a lawyer and judge of Lima. During the terrible earthquake of 1746 he had worked with such skill and courage that he had been put in charge of the treasures which had been brought out of the ruins, and was trusted to restore their belongings to people who could bring satisfactory claims. Out of that which he believed could not be claimed he built a church and a theatre; but naturally there were some disgruntled people who accused him of cheating, and as a result he was imprisoned for a while and made to pay certain sums of money.

After that he left Lima, married a rich woman and travelled to Europe. Arriving in France, he found the atmosphere of a country tottering on the brink of revolution extremely interesting, and he quickly became the friend of Voltaire and Rousseau.

Imbued with their ideas of bettering the conditions of the starving multitude he returned to Spain. Although he was a philosopher he was – as is seen by his activities at the time of the earthquake – a practical man, and he soon made a plan of action.

There were in the country great tracts of land which was useless except for sheep-grazing and was used by a band of people called the *Mesta* who owned sheep which wandered from place to place grazing on this uncultivated land – the *baldios* as it was called. They had secured the right to use this land and to prevent its being cultivated.

It had for some time been realized that this land could be put to useful service, and it was decided to bring into the country German and Swiss Catholics to cultivate the waste land. Olavide was made superintendent of the colony and governor of Seville.

This was to bring him many enemies, not only among the *Mesta* who hated him for spoiling their grazing grounds, but among the friars who had accompanied the colonists, for Olavide had become imbued with ideas from France, liberal ideas which seemed like heresy to the bigoted priests.

The charges brought against him were that, when calamity threatened, he did not pray but used practical means to avert it; he did not order that bells should be rung when storms rose; he supported the Copernican statement that the sun was the centre of the solar system, which it was against the command of the Church to believe.

In earlier days Olavide would have quickly been a prisoner of the Inquisition, but with the changing times caution was needed; and it was necessary to obtain royal permission before an arrest could be made.

This consent was given – very probably because the King realized that the ideas, which Olavide held and which he was no doubt circulating, were those of his friends Voltaire and Rousseau and, although he could not yet see the disaster this was to bring to his relations in Versailles, Charles was clever enough to scent danger in them.

Olavide was arrested in November 1776 and for two years

nothing was heard of him. Meanwhile many witnesses were brought before the Tribunal in order to build up a case against him, and at length one hundred and sixty-six possible charges were drawn up. Olavide admitted that he had talked freely, but he denied that he was not a Catholic.

The Inquisition would have preferred him to be paraded in a public *auto de fé* as a warning to others who might be dabbling in new ideas. Yet again here is an example of their waning power. Instructions came from Rome that the *auto* should not be a public one, so it was held in an outer court of the Inquisition of Madrid without the banners and trumpetings of the past, and instead of the hysterical crowd, a mere sixty spectators – all of high rank and many of whom had already been flirting with the new ideas.

Olavide dressed in black serge and holding an unlighted torch in his hand was commanded to march three times round the court, although he was excused from wearing the *sanbenito* and rope round his neck.

He was then obliged to listen to a recital of his crimes which lasted for three hours; he cried out that it was wrong to say he had lost faith. These interruptions were ignored. As a great favour he was allowed to sit on a bench while his sentence was read to him.

Under Philip II it would have been the stake for him; in these more enlightened days he was given a less severe sentence, but it was none the less a very harsh one – so harsh that when Olavide heard it he fell from his bench in a faint.

He was accused of being a heretic and a bad member of Holy Church; therefore he must be reconciled and suffer confiscation of his goods; he was to be banished, for as long as he lived, from Madrid, nor must he come within forty leagues of the city, all royal residences, Andalusia, Lima and the colonies of Sierra Morena which he had recently governed. For eight years he was to suffer strict imprisonment in a convent, where he would occupy a cell and take orders from a confessor who would be appointed to him by the Inquisition. He was never to ride on horseback again, or wear jewels, gold, silver, diamonds or pearls or any precious stones. His garments must never be made of silk or fine wool, but always of coarse serge.

Two years after the sentence was passed he became so ill in his prison that he was allowed to leave it for a short respite, and he then escaped to France. It is said that many at Court were aware of his intended flight and were sympathetic towards him. The Inquisition, however, demanded that he be brought back to serve his sentence, and Olavide thought it safer to go to Geneva.

He returned to Paris when the revolution broke out but doubtless found it different from what he had anticipated; indeed he himself narrowly escaped death by the guillotine; and no doubt realizing that revolution in practice was very different from revolution in theory he wrote his *The Gospel Triumphant; or the Converted Philosopher*, which so impressed the Inquisitors that they graciously allowed him to return to his native land.

He died in 1804, a disillusioned man, it is said.

The case of Olavide was considered by the Inquisition to have been an important one because it provided a lesson to many who were dabbling in the new ideas. It was for this reason that many suspected of harbouring them were invited to see Olavide condemned; and one of these, Don Felipe Samaniego, who was Archdeacon of Pampeluna, confessed immediately that he had read literature concerning the new ideas; and during an investigation of his case suspicion was levied at many of the King's ministers. These cases, however, remained suspended on the grounds that only one witness had been found to testify against the accused. This clearly indicates the waning power of the Inquisition which in the past had never failed to find terrified witnesses ready to testify against those whom it was desired to prosecute.

The end of the Inquisition was in sight, although it was to continue for some years. In spite of war which overshadowed the reign of Charles III, he left Spain a richer country than he found her. The population had increased considerably, taxation had diminished although revenues had increased. Spain began to be famous for the leather of Seville and Cordova, for the cotton-velvet of Avila, for the glass of La Granja, and the porcelain of Buen Retiro. Agriculture revived, the coinage was reformed; marshes were drained and arid lands irrigated;

canals and roads were built. If the monarchs who succeeded Charles III had been of his calibre there would have been every chance of Spain's rising to become a great power once more.

Charles III died in December 1788; he was seventy-three years of age, but the temperate life he had lived had preserved his strength and vigour; the twenty-nine years, during which this intelligent and just king had ruled, were indeed a boon to the long-suffering country.

CHAPTER NINETEEN

# DECLINE AND FALL

Unfortunately Charles IV was very different from his father, Charles III, and, while his intentions were good, he was weak, lazy and considerably under the influence of his forceful wife, Maria Luisa of Parma, who was not even faithful to him, but was, in her turn, strongly influenced by her lover, the ambitious Manuel Godoy.

As Charles IV came to the throne in 1788, the revolution was about to break over France, and since the coming of the Bourbons there had been a strong affinity between the two countries.

A censorship was imposed on all literature coming in from France, and the Inquisition began to regain some of the importance it had lost. Yet, as is seen in the case of the favourite, Manuel Godoy, it was not gaining any real strength with the passing years.

Godoy's relationship with the imperious Queen was deeply resented by her son, the Prince of the Asturias, and when there was an intrigue to bring about the fall of Godoy, the Inquisition was appealed to as the most likely means of achieving this.

Godoy was accused of his immorality with women and the fact that he did not observe ordinary religious duties such as communion and confession. Inquisitor-General Francisco Antonio de Lorenzana, Archbishop of Toledo, was very wary of attacking the favourite, hesitated and would not take action unless he could first receive the permission of the Pope, Pius VI, to do so. The Archbishop Despuig of Seville, who was one of the instigators of the plot against Godoy, with his friend Cardinal Vincenti, begged the Pope to write to the Inquisitor-General reprimanding him for having failed in his duty towards such a sinner as Godoy. Napoleon, who was in Genoa, captured the messenger and the letter, and sent it to Godoy, for the Corsican adventurer was well aware of the power Godoy held in Spain and how useful he might be.

Godoy was therefore aware of the conspirators' aims, and sent them, with the Inquisitor-General, into exile.

With the French monarchy abolished and Napoleon striding across Europe, it was small wonder that the Inquisition felt its position to be growing more and more uneasy. Yet it was prodded to fresh bursts of energy by the fear of revolutionary ideas, spreading to Spain from France; and at this time it became more an instrument of the state than one for suppressing heresy; which was, at this time, its surest way of keeping itself intact.

When the French and English were at war it was necessary for Spain to take sides, and after Godoy had signed the Treaty of San Ildefonso, England declared war on Spain. The result was defeat for the Spaniards off Cape St Vincent and the loss of Trinidad; and later the great battle of Trafalgar was fought, when Nelson destroyed both French and Spanish fleets.

When Napoleon realized that he could not beat the British by force of arms he determined to do so by economic blockade, and insisted that all European ports should be closed to British shipping. Because Portugal refused to comply, Napoleon planned to use force against her, and it was arranged that the armies of Spain and France should together conquer Portugal.

When Napoleon seized the opportunity of sending troops to Spain this naturally caused some concern in Madrid. The Prince of the Asturias had been imprisoned for taking part in the plot against Godoy and there were riots in the capital, the result of which was the desired abdication of Charles IV in favour of Fernando VII, Prince of the Asturias.

Napoleon then summoned Charles and Fernando to Bayonne where he insisted that they renounce the throne in favour of his, Napoleon's brother Joseph.

Thus began the War of Independence, with Spain in revolt against the French. In December 1808 Madrid capitulated to Napoleon, and when the Emperor reached the city he suppressed the Inquisition because he considered it against civic authority and sovereignty, and at the same time confiscated its property.

The members of the Supreme Council escaped from Madrid in spite of the fact that Napoleon had ordered them to be imprisoned; and although they were unable to keep in communication with the Pope, they managed to set up tribunals in those parts of Spain not yet in French hands.

The Inquisitors were now more concerned with keeping their freedom than prosecuting for heresy, and Lea quotes the archives of Valencia as giving the total number of cases brought before all the tribunals in 1808 as 67; in 1809, 22; in 1810, 17; in 1811, 25; in 1812, 1; and in 1813, 6.

Stories of the barbarous conduct of the Inquisition were now circulated throughout the world. Instruments of torture, which the invading armies had discovered, were described in all their horrible detail. There is a story that the French, entering the Palace of the Inquisition at Madrid, were greeted with great courtesy by the Inquisitors and shown the building from top to bottom, being assured that the stories of brutalities were gross exaggerations. One of the French officers, after having searched in vain for the dungeons of which he had heard, had the flagstones of the great hall taken up, and there below the floor discovered the cells and torture chambers which had been described. The French were reputed to have found victims still living among the dead. It was on this occasion that soldiers were said to have discovered that instrument of torture known as the Iron Virgin – an image of the Virgin Mary the front of which was covered with sharp nails and daggers. The arms of this image could be moved to draw a victim close until the body of that victim was pierced by the nails and daggers.

The story of Napoleon's disasters is well known; and how when he turned his attention to Russia he found defeat. His brother Joseph could not hold Madrid, for Wellington had brought his military genius into the field.

Joseph was forced to return to France and the War of Independence was over. But the Napoleonic invasion of Spain had brought with it new ideas as to the constitution; previously the King had reigned supreme; now the Council of Castile governed, but without much success; and *juntas* appeared in various parts of the country.

The Church party sought to bring back the Inquisition, and

there was a long and heated debate in the Cortes; and finally it was decided that the Inquisition was not compatible with the Constitution. The Church party wailed that the Catholic Faith – and Christianity itself – was at stake. But the liberals were triumphant, and their manifesto stated that the Inquisition, which had been guilty of many abuses, was responsible for the decline in the fortune of Spain. They returned the right to judge religious crimes to the bishops.

During this time Fernando had been living in exile at Valençay, virtually the prisoner of Napoleon who had allowed him to live a life of ease, giving him all the privileges he asked except to ride on horseback. Napoleon is reputed to have kept him well supplied with handsome women, for Fernando was very fond of them; and for these benefits Fernando had been ready to obey Napoleon.

Fernando now returned to Madrid, and everywhere he was greeted with jubilation, for the people believed that with the coming of the King their troubles were at an end.

The people of Spain did not know their King. Idle, debauched, he was treacherous and quite incapable of the great task which lay before him. In the first place he wished to return to absolute monarchy and was not prepared to be guided by the Cortes.

He declared that he would not accept the new constitution and that any who upheld it were guilty of treason, the reward of which was death. Tyranny returned; arrests were made; and those who opposed the King's will were imprisoned and tortured; and on 21st July, 1814, Fernando declared that the Holy Office should be revived, and Xavier de Mier y Campillo, Bishop of Almería, became Inquisitor-General.

Fernando might believe he could return to the old despotic days, but liberalism had come to Spain and it was not easily suppressed. During the next years revolution was continually threatening to break out, and in 1820 Rafael de Riego, the commander of a battalion of the Asturias, incited his men to rebellion. Revolution swept through Spain and everywhere men and women were declaring their desire for the return to the constitutional method of government.

Fernando, the coward, readily took the oath to the Constitution when he saw that he could do nothing else; and after that the bells rang for three nights, and the people stormed the prisons of the Inquisition and set prisoners free. Fernando did as he was commanded and issued an order abolishing the Inquisition.

Those who were determined to uphold the Inquisition watched the revolution with trepidation, knowing that should it prove entirely successful the days of the Holy Office were numbered.

The new government was not successful in maintaining peace throughout the country, and Spain was in chaos. The King, although still recognized as King, was a captive, and the French, under Louis XIV's nephew, the Duc d'Angoulême, chose the opportunity to invade on pretext of restoring the monarchy.

The French campaign was successful inasmuch as Fernando was restored to his kingdom. One of his first acts was to restore the conditions which were existing before 1820, and which included the re-establishment of the Inquisition. His next was to give full vent to his vindictiveness, and the prisons were full of his enemies who were maltreated in every conceivable way.

The French however were opposed to the return of the Inquisition, and Fernando, whose great desire was to be an absolute monarch, was uncertain whether the Inquisition might not curb his ambitions; he realized also that to restore an Institution which was being universally condemned throughout Europe would be an unwise act.

The bishops continued with the work of the Inquisition under the name of *juntas de fé*; they used similar methods to those used by the Inquisitors, and these were even more to be feared than the Inquisition itself had been in later years because there was no Supreme Council to keep an eye on what was going on. Yet there were still many who clamoured for the return of the Inquisition.

On 26th July, 1826, Cayetano Ripoll, a schoolmaster of Rizaffa, met his death. During the war he had been made a prisoner and taken to France where he had become interested in new ideas, and had turned from Christianity to Deism. He had lived very simply, following the teaching of Christ, sharing everything he had with others. He believed that it was not necessary to go to Mass, and all that mattered was that people should do to others as they would be done by.

It was reported to the Inquisition that he and his scholars used the ejaculation 'Praise be to God' instead of '*Ave Maria purissima*', that he did not insist on his scholars going to Mass and kneeling to the Viaticum. It was also brought against him that the only religious teaching he deemed necessary was the keeping of the Ten Commandments.

He was arrested in 1824 and kept in prison for two years, during which time attempts were made to force him to admit his errors. This he refused to do.

The Tribunal and the *junta de fé* finally judged him to be a heretic, and he was sentenced to be hanged and burned. He was duly hanged, but owing to the changed opinion of these times the burning was to be a matter of form, and the body of the schoolmaster was merely put into a barrel which had flames painted upon it. In this barrel he was buried in unconsecrated ground.

The execution of this truly pious schoolmaster was discussed throughout Europe, and there were shocked comments on the barbarities still practised in Spain.

The schoolmaster of Rizaffa has become famous for being the last victim executed for heresy.

In 1833 Fernando VII died and, as he himself said, the cork was removed from the fermenting and surcharged bottle of Spain. The following year the Inquisition was finally suppressed.

The *juntas de fé* continued to exist, but the old Inquisitorial customs had no place in the modern world, and in 1835 the Regent, Queen Cristina, commanded that they should be immediately abolished. With this order that Institution, which had brought so much misery to countless thousands and had played a leading part in the destruction of a mighty empire, was no more. The fire of Torquemada, the piety of Isabella, the cupidity of Ferdinand, the zeal of Ximenes, the bigotry of Philip II, had contributed to its monstrous power, but now it was dead – brought to its ignoble end by the enlightenment of a new era.

# INQUISITORS-GENERAL – FROM THE RISE OF THE SPANISH INQUISITION TO ITS SUPPRESSION

Tomás de Torquemada, 1483–98.
Miguel de Morillo shared Inquisitor-Generalship in 1491.

*In 1494 the following additional Inquisitors-General were appointed:*
Martin Ponce de Leon, Archbishop of Messina. Died 1500.
Iñigo Manrique, Bishop of Córdova. Died 1496.
Francisco Sánchez de la Fuente, Bishop of Avila. Died 1498.
Alonso Suárez de Fuentelsaz, Bishop of Jaen. Resigned 1504. Died 1520.

*Appointed in 1498:*
Diego Deza, Archbishop of Seville. Appointed for Castile, Leon and Granada. In 1499 appointed for all Spain. Resigned 1507. Died 1523.

*Inquisitions of Castile and Aragon separated.*

## Castile

Francisco Ximenes de Cisneros, Cardinal and Archbishop of Toledo, 1507–17.

## Aragon

Juan Enguera, Bishop of Vich and Lérida, 1507–13.
Luis Mercader, Bishop of Tortosa. 1513–16.
Juan Pedro de Poul, commissioned 1516, died 1516.
Adrian of Utrecht, Cardinal and Bishop of Tortosa, appointed 1516.

*The Inquisitions of Castile and Aragon were then united.*
Adrian of Utrecht was Inquisitor-General until he was elected to the Papacy. 1522.

Alfonso Manrique, Cardinal and Archbishop of Seville, 1523–38.

Juan Pardo de Tavera, Cardinal and Archbishop of Toledo, 1539–45.

Francisco García de Loaysa, Archbishop of Seville, February 1546–April 1546.

Fernando Valdés, Archbishop of Seville, 1547. Resigned 1566, died 1568.

Diego Espinosa, Cardinal and Bishop of Sigüenza. 1566–72.

Pedro Ponce de Leon y Córdova, Bishop of Plasencia, appointed 1572. His brief arrived after his death, 1573.

Gaspar de Quiroga, Cardinal and Archbishop of Toledo, 1573–94.

Gerónimo Manrique de Lara, Bishop of Avila, August to November 1595.

Pedro de Portocarrero, Bishop of Cuenca, 1596. Resigned 1599. Died 1600.

Fernando Niño de Guevara, Cardinal and Archbishop of Seville, 1599. Resigned 1602. Died 1609.

Juan de Zuñiga, Bishop of Cartagena, July to December 1602.

Juan Bautista Acevedo, 1603–8.

Bernardo de Sandoval y Roxas, Cardinal and Archbishop of Toledo, 1608–18.

Luis de Aliaga, 1619. Resigned 1621. Died 1626.

Andrés Pacheco, Bishop of Cuenca, 1622–26.

Antonio de Zapata, Cardinal and Archbishop of Burgos, 1627. Resigned 1632. Died 1635.

Antonio de Sotomayor, Archbishop of Damascus, 1632. Resigned 1643. Died 1648.

Diego de Arce y Reynoso, Bishop of Plasencia, 1643–65.

Pascual de Aragon, Archbishop of Toledo, 1665.

Juan Everardo Nithard, 1666. Vanished 1669. Died 1681.

Diego Sarmiento de Valladares, Bishop of Plasencia, 1669–95.

Juan Tomás de Rocaberti, Archbishop of Valencia, 1695–99.

Alfonso Fernández de Cordova y Aguilar. Died September 1699 before his brief arrived.

Balthasar de Mendoza y Sandoval, Bishop of Segovia, 1699. Resigned 1705. Died 1727.

Vidal Marin, Bishop of Ceuta 1705–9.

Antonio Ybañez de la Riva-Herrer, Archbishop of Saragossa 1709–10.

Francesco Giudice, 1711. Resigned 1716. Died 1725.

Felipe Antonio Gil de Taboada. Appointed 1715 but did not serve.

Josef de Molines. Appointed 1717 while in Rome. Died in Milan on way home to his appointment.

Juan de Arzamendi. Died without serving.

Diego de Astorga y Cespedes, Bishop of Barcelona, 1720. Resigned 1720. Died 1724.

Juan de Camargo, Bishop of Pampeluna, 1720–33.

Andrés de Orbe y Larreategui, Archbishop of Valencia, 1733–40.

Manuel Isidro Manrique de Lara, Archbishop of Santiago, 1742–6.

Francisco Pérez de Prado y Cuesta, Bishop of Teruel, 1746–55.

Manuel Quintano Bonifaz, Archbishop of Pharsalia, 1775. Resigned 1774. Died 1775.

Felipe Beltran, Bishop of Salamanca, 1775–83.

Agustin Rubin de Cevallos, Bishop of Jaen, 1784–93.

Manuel Abad y la Sierra, Archbishop of Selimbria, 1793. Resigned 1794. Died 1806.

Francisco Antonio de Lorenzana, Archbishop of Toledo, 1794. Resigned 1797. Died 1804.

Ramon Josef de Arce y Reynoso, Archbishop of Saragossa, 1798. Resigned 1808. Died 1814.

Xavier Mier y Campillo, Bishop of Almería, 1814–18.

Gerónimo Castellon y Salas, Bishop of Tarazona. 1818–34. The last Inquisitor-General.

# PRINCIPAL WORKS CONSULTED

Acton, John Emerich Edward Dalberg, First Baron Acton, D.C.L., LL.D., Edited with an introduction by John Neville Figgis, M.A., and Reginald Vere Laurence, M.A. *The History of Freedom and Other Essays* (1907)

Adams, Nicholson B. *The Heritage of Spain: An Introduction to Spanish Civilization* (1949)

Alberti, L. de, and Chapman, A. B. Wallis, D.Sc. (Econ.) (Edited by). *English Merchants and the Spanish Inquisition in the Canaries.* Extracts from the Archives in the Possession of the Most Hon. The Marquess of Bute (1912)

Aradi, Zsolt. *The Popes* (1956)

Aubrey, William Hickman Smith. *The National and Domestic History of England*

Bainton, Roland H. *The Reformation of the 16th Century* (1953)

Bainton, Roland H. *The Travail of Religious Liberty* (1953)

Baker, The Rev, J., M.A. (Compiled and Translated by). *The History of the Inquisition as it subsists in the Kingdoms of Spain, Portugal, etc., and both the Indies to this day* (1734)

Berdyaev, Nicolas. With a Commentary and Notes by Alan A. Spears. Translated by Alan A. Spears and Victor B. Kanter. *Christianity and Anti-Semitism* (1952)

Bertrand, Louis and Sir Charles Petrie, M.A., F.R.Hist.S. *The History of Spain* (1934)

Bury, J. B. with an Epilogue by H. J. Blackham. *A History of Freedom of Thought* (1952)

Butterfield, Herbert. *Christianity in European History* (1951)

Cary-Elwes, Columbia, Monk of Ampleforth. With a preface by Professor Arnold Toynbee. *Law, Liberty and Love* (1949)

Creighton, M., D.D. Oxon. and Cam. *Persecution and Tolerance* (1895)

Dawson, Christopher. *Religion and the Rise of Western Culture* (1950)

Deanesly, M., M.A. *A History of the Medieval Church 590–1500* (1925)

Gifford, William Alva. *The Story of the Faith. A survey of Christian History for the Undogmatic* (1946)

Gordon, Janet. *The Spanish Inquisition* (1898)

Gowen, Herbert H., D.D., F.R.A.S. *A History of Religion* (1934)

Guizot, M. Translated by Robert Black, M.A. *The History of France* (1881)

Hume, Martin A. S. Revised by Edward Armstrong. *Spain: Its Greatness and Decay (1479/1788) Cambridge Historical Series* (1931)

Hume, Martin A. S. *The Court of Philip IV. Spain in Decadence* (1907)

Hume, Martin A. S. *Queens of Old Spain* (1906)

Lea, Henry Charles, LL.D. *A History of the Inquisition of the Middle ages.* 3 Volumes (1887)

Lea, Henry Charles, LL.D. *A History of the Inquisition of Spain.* 4 Volumes (1908)

Lea, Henry Charles, LL.D. *Chapters from the Religious History of Spain connected with the Inquisition* (1890)

Lea, Henry Charles, LL.D. *Superstition and Forces* (1892)

Lea, Henry Charles, LL.D. The Inquisition in the Spanish Dependencies (1908)

Limborch, Philip. *The History of the Inquisition* (1816)

Marañón, Gregorio, Translated from the Spanish by Charles David Ley. *Antonio Pérez 'Spanish Traitor'* (1954)

Marchant, John, and others. *A review of the Bloody Tribunal; or the Horrid Cruelties of the Inquisition as practised in Spain, Portugal, Italy and the East and West Indies* (1770)

Maycock, A. L., M.A. With an Introduction by Father Ronald Knox. *The Inquisition from its Establishment to the Great Schism* (1926)

McKinnon, James, Ph.D., D.D., D.Th., LL.D. *Calvin and the Reformation* (1936)

McKnight, John P. *The Papacy* (1953)

Mortimer, R. C., M.A., B.D. *The Elements of Moral Theology* (1947)

Nickerson, Hoffman. With a Preface by Hilaire Belloc. *The Inquisition. A Political and Military Study of its Establishment* (1923)

Presscott, William H. *History of the Reign of Ferdinand and Isabella the Catholic.* 2 Volumes.

Presscott, William H. *History of the Reign of Philip II, King of Spain.* 3 Volumes (1873)

Poole Reginald Lane. *Illustrations of the History of Medieval Thought and Learning* (1880)

Robertson, John M. *A Short History of Freethought Ancient and Modern.* 2 Volumes (1915)

Roth, Cecil. *The Spanish Inquisition* (1937)

Rule, William Harris, D.D. *History of the Inquisition.* 2 Volumes (1874)

Shewring, Walter. (Translated and Introduced by) *Rich and Poor in Christian Tradition. Writings of many centuries* (1947)

Simon, Dr Paul, Translated from the German by Meyrick Booth, Ph.D. *The Human Element in the Church of Christ* (1953)

Stephen, James Fitzjames, Q.C. *Liberty, Equality, Fraternity* (1873)

Swain, John. *The Pleasures of the Torture Chamber* (1931)

Turberville, A. S., M.C., M.A., B.Litt. *The Spanish Inquisition* (1932)

Turberville, A. S., M.C., M.A., B.Litt. *Medieval Heresy and the Inquisition* (1920)

Wiseman, F. J., M.A. *Roman Spain. An introduction to the Roman Antiquities of Spain and Portugal* (1956)

*The Catholic Encyclopedia: An International Work of Reference on the Constitution, Doctrine, Discipline and History of the Catholic Church.* Edited by Charles G. Herbermann, Ph.D., LL.D.; Edward A. Pace, Ph.D., D.D.; Condé B, Pallen, Ph.D., LL.D.; Thomas J. Shahan, D.D.; John J. Wynne, S. J. Assisted by numerous collaborators (1907)

# INDEX

Philip II, – *contd*
lands, 14; Alva's letters to him, 15; seeks to justify Alva's conduct, 16; questions wisdom of Alva's rule, 17; attitude to English sailors, bigotry, 19, 32; sets up Inquisition in Mexico, 35; Inquisition and politics, Philip's devious ways, 37; involvement in Pérez case, 39, 40, 41; suspicions of Don John, 45; gives orders for murder of Escobedo, 47; possible lover of Princess of Éboli, 48; orders arrest of Pérez and the Princess, 49; vindictiveness, 50; calls in Inquisition to deal with Pérez, 51; fury against Pérez, 53; oath regarding constitution of Aragon, use of Inquisition against Jeanne of Navarre, anxieties over Don Carlos, 54, 55; Carlos plans to murder him, 56; death, 57; orders Don John to crush Moorish revolt, 61; offered bribe by Moors, 62; sentiments regarding Catholic Faith, 66; his letters read in Mexico, 69; Luis López writes critical pamphlet, 98; asks Gregory XIII for financial help, 107; attempts to set up Inquisition in Milan, 108; conquers Portugal and attempts to bring Portuguese Inquisition under Spanish rule, 111; his simple faith, 122; lack of extravagance at his Court, 123; insistence on unity of faith, 143; population in his time, 156; his religious fervour, 168; severity during his reign, 174; bigotry, 182

Philip III, 6; indulgence to Pérez, 54; condition of Spain at his ascension to throne, 58; asked to abolish Inquisition, 59; alarmed by Moorish plot, 63; Lamport's claims, 71, 72; needs of Inquisition in Sardinia during his reign, 106; character, 122; decline of country under his reign, 123; visit to Portugal, sickness, 124; death, 125; ruffs worn during his reign, 131, 158

Philip IV, 6; Lamport's allegations, 71, 122; Moorish rising on day of birth, 123; ceremonial visit to Portugal, encouraged in sexual adventures, marriage, 124; becomes king, generosity, sensuality, jealousy of Queen, 126; love of pleasure, birth of two children, 127; present at *auto* of 4th July, 1624, 129; under influence of Olivares, 130; illness, conscience, love affair with Maria Calderon, 133; at war, 135; dismisses Olivares, 135; meets Sor Maria de Agreda and seeks to reform, 137; attitude to Inquisition, influence of Sor Maria, 140; grief at loss of son, 138; marries again, tires of wife, birth of son, 141; sickness, melancholy, 141; death, Inquisition at height of power,

Wyndham Books are obtainable from many booksellers and newsagents. If you have any difficulty please send purchase price plus postage on the scale below to:

**Wyndham Cash Sales,**
**PO Box 11,**
**Falmouth,**
**Cornwall.**

OR

**Star Book Service,**
**G.P.O. Box 29,**
**Douglas,**
**Isle of Man,**
**British Isles.**

While every effort is made to keep prices low, it is sometimes necessary to increase prices at short notice. Wyndham Books reserve the right to show new retail prices on covers which may differ from those advertised in the text or elsewhere.

**Postage and Packing Rate**
**U.K.**
One book 22p plus 10p per copy for each additional book ordered to a maximum charge of 82p.

**B.F.P.O. & Eire**
One book 22p plus 10p per copy for the next 6 books, and thereafter 4p per book.

**Overseas**
One book 30p plus 10p per copy for each additional book.

These charges are subject to Post Office charge fluctuations